J.E. CHARLTON

JECharlton

COINMAN
TO
CANADIANS

**PREPARED FROM THE CHARLTON PAPERS,
CORRESPONDENCE AND CONVERSATIONS
BY
H. DON ALLEN**

**INCORPORATING 80 YEARS
OF ILLUSTRATIONS**

**W. K. CROSS
PUBLISHER**

The Charlton Press

TORONTO, ONTARIO ▶ PALM HARBOR, FLORIDA

The National Library of Canada has catalogued this publication as follows:

Allen, Harold Don, 1931-
  J. E. Charlton : coinman to Canadians
Includes bibliographical references.
ISBN 0-88968-142-2
  1. Charlton, J. E., 1911- 2. Coin dealers—Canada—Biography.
3. Numismatics—Collectors and collecting—Canada—History—20th
century. I. Title
CJ1867.A44 2001   381'.45737'092   C2001-901698-0

Printed in Canada
in the Province of Ontario

The Charlton Press

Editorial Office
2040 Yonge Street, Suite 208, Toronto, Ontario, N4S 1Z9
Telephone: (416) 488-1418 Fax: (416) 488-4656
Telephone: (800) 442-6042 Fax: (800) 442-1542
Web Site: www.charltonpress.com;
E-mail: chpress@charltonpress.com

CONTENTS

PART I – MY GOOD FRIEND, THE COINMAN 1

PART II - RECOLLECTIONS AND REFLECTIONS OF JAMES E. CHARLTON
1. The Formative Years (To 1933)..35
2. Northern Ontario Commitments (1933-1948) 51
3. Toronto, *The Star*, and the Coin Business 59
4. Catalogues ... and Numismatic Periodicals..73
5. The Canadian Numismatic Scene 91
6. Personalities — and Great Friends — in Numismatics 105
7. Interests ... and Adventures 123
8. Florida ... and Relative Retirement 137
9. After Five Decades...141
10. In Conclusion 153

APPENDICES
A. James Edward Charlton: A Chronology 157
B. Jim Charlton and Organized Numismatics 159
C. Jim's First 47 Canadian Conventions 161
D. Some Relevant Canadian Readings 162
E. Price List of Sheldon S. Carroll, 1938 164
F. Canada Coin Exchange, Price List, 1949..168
G. Canada Coin Exchange, Selected Offerings, 1951 170
H. Convention Auction Highlights, 1954 173
I. CANTEL Teletype Circuit Membership..175
J. Canada Coin Exchange Commercial, CKFH, 1963 177
K. Jim Charlton's Auctions, 1950-1969 178
L. Pricing of Selected Coins, 1952-2002...179

BIBLIOGRAPHY...185

1953 CATALOGUE OF

CANADIAN

COINS, TOKENS

&

FRACTIONAL CURRENCY

2nd Edition

BY J. E. CHARLTON

Published By

CANADA COIN EXCHANGE
BOX 35, TERMINAL A
TORONTO, CANADA

PRINTED IN CANADA

1953 Catalogue of Canadian Coins, Tokens & Fractional Currency, 2nd Edition

I

My Good Friend, the Coinman

"Mr. Coin Will Visit Gananoque."

The yellowed clipping from a Kingston and district paper dates back nearly four decades, to November of 1963.

The Gananoque Coin Club, marking its first anniversary, would be expecting 75 coin enthusiasts from the Gananoque, Belleville, Brockville, Athens, Elgin, and Watertown, N.Y., area, at a dinner meeting. The invited guest speaker — and after-dinner auctioneer — would be "Toronto's 'Mr. Coin,'" the newspaper asserted.

Close to four decades later — is there still a Gananoque Coin Club? — the guest speaker still would require no further identification.

"Toronto's 'Mr. Coin'" would have been, and still is, James E. (Jim) Charlton. Jim, through a generation of priced coin catalogues that he produced and published (1952-1980) and the succeeding Charlton Press editions that well perpetuate his name, and through a great range of other business and promotional activities, brought popular numismatics — the "coin hobby" to Canadians, as no one had before.

Jim's unstinting efforts also served, not incidentally, to make aspects of Canadian numismatics — coins, tokens, paper money — more known and sought outside the country than ever had been the case.

Americans, in truth, find it useful to think of Jim Charlton as "Canada's Dick Yeoman" — recalling the Red Book author, their country's foremost recent numismatic cataloguer and popularizer. The comparison is sound. Jim's catalogues, newspaper columns, television appearances, and coin club talks brought Canadian numismatics to — quite literally — the millions, both in Canada and beyond. This continued for well over 20 years, then Jim opted for a long-planned retirement. That, in turn, was over 30 years ago. Making — and extending — a unique contribution to the leisure life of Canadians, Jim, after turn of millennium, is still going strong!

Jim called me a while back, virtually the day I got off the plane from a four-year stint of education work in Canada's Eastern Arctic. He offered me access to his papers — a mountain of them! — and invited me to take on the task of sharing their content with interested readers.

You're now looking at the result.

This is the story of Jim Charlton. Jim was — and is — an extraordinary figure in North American numismatics. What you read and view here may offer insights into who Jim is, and why he is the way he is.

The story is Jim's story, necessarily played out against the backdrop of Canada's twentieth century numismatic stage.

I've known Jim a long time.

Well over 40 years.

On more than one occasion, I've been privileged to support Jim in getting out his incredible Catalogues or in presenting them on publication.

When first I actually met Jim, he was doing what he certainly does best, auctioning fine material at a national numismatic convention — the Canadian Numismatic Association, at Ottawa's Chateau Laurier, in early September, 1958. Jim sold me the one item that I bid on, a Newfoundland Government 1913-14 "dual date" one dollar note, "payable at the Bank of Montreal." A stiff price — $25.00, in 1958 dollars. I derive pleasure from that note to this day. A surviving press photo of Jim at that early convention depicts him "fanning" a group of such older bills that were about to be up for bids. My black and green Newfoundland Government Cash Note I think I can see in that shot!

As often is the case in a context such as numismatics, Jim and I had known each other quite well by correspondence before we finally met. Some mass-market numismatic popularization that I'd authored (References 3, 6) had ultimately involved Jim, as a numismatic professional; and had encouraged him toward such numismatic newspaper writing, I like to think.

That was 1958, and earlier.

Numismatics is a whole world, we all realize. I soon found my preferred numismatic niche in particularly fine organizations in the United States and overseas, and my annual pleasant encounters with Jim tended to be at American Numismatics Association gatherings, or at specialized groups that opt to meet where and when A.N.A. meets — groups such as the Organization of International Numismatists (Reference 9), International Bank Note Society, Society of Paper Money Collectors, Tokens and Medals Society, Check Collectors Round Table, and Society of Ration Token Collectors. Boston, Philadelphia, New Orleans, Miami Beach, Los Angeles, New York City, Atlanta, St. Louis, Detroit ... on the huge and crowded bourse floor or in a general meeting, Jim's very often was the first familiar Canadian face that I'd spot.

My first Charlton Catalogue I bought from Phil Spier, the "coin man" at Spier Brothers, then on Montreal's Craig Street, at the time a pawn shop area. (The occasional numismatic "find" could derive from the M. Mendelson pawn shop, down the block by Montreal Tramways' wondrous Terminus Craig.) Spiers' had a well-worn 1902 $4 note in their window, at a $10 price. I wasn't tempted. It was more fun, and much more satisfying, to chase down such items at face. Spiers' subsequently moved to a more upscale location at 1817A St. Catherine Street West, back when St. Catherine Street was more upscale. It would have been a 20 minute walk from where Breton did business (now a parking lot). The Spiers' location is a new and used bookstore at this time.

Each year I acquired a new "Charlton." Grades and prices didn't interest me, but statistics — as in mintage figures — did. I wanted to be current, and there was the hope that a new catalogue would offer new insights, which frequently it did.

Some years ago, Dan Gosling, an Edmonton collector, inaugurated a web site on Jim and his catalogues. He recently downloaded for me a detailed review of Jim's Eighth Edition, which I'd written for *The Numismatist* of December 1959. Time passes!

We shall return to Dan Gosling in a few pages.

Near the peak of the Sixties coin enthusiasm, I had a loose affiliation with Montreal's highly-regarded English-language A.M. outlet, CJAD. Jim, and others, appeared with me to "talk coins" on the occasion of a major Montreal show.

Burglars took coins as a consolation prize in a very professional break-in at a large high school where I advised youthful coin enthusiasts. Jim came to the rescue, in what I think of as a characteristic act. Coin sets, books, and other collector items constituted the club's educational exhibit in a locked display window. Treasured by its owners, but not the stuff to motivate a break-in by pros. The burglars, rather, were after school fees, thousands of dollars, and they crashed through a wall into a walk-in vault. Zilch! Fees were banked daily. The break-in, however, had two unfortunate side effects. The burglars took the students' coins. And the vault had contained the schools forthcoming term examinations, all of which (to be sure) had to be reset. Jim quietly replaced the stolen coins. The youngsters were delighted. I've not had reason to mention this before.

Jim and I next crossed paths in the Chibougamau mining fields, a Quebec area (formerly Rupert's Land) not unlike the Northern Ontario in which Jim had put in such good years. The setting was an improbable one, a licensed non-commercial broadcasting station, CHIB, with a war surplus transmitter and an improvised studio up above the "Rec Centre" gymnasium at Pine Tree Line R.C.A.F. Station Chibougamau. A group of us staged a weekly Coin Club on the Air — see *Canadian Numismatic Journal*, January 1964, p. 13 — and Jim was our featured guest, by telephone interview. The community also developed an excellent little regular coin club, meeting at odd hours in the local motion picture theatre — the manager was a particularly active collector. More informal meetings were in the post office lobby, when mail had been sorted and newly-arrived treasures made for a spritely show and tell.

So much "water under the bridge"? Not entirely. Some fine Canadian numismatists had their start in such modest beginnings, a leading researcher having had his boyhood nickels restored after the Montreal school break-in, and a well-established Atlantic Canada dealer having been a boyhood participant in Chibougamau get-togethers.

And what, I ask old friends, has become of T. Richard Masuda? Dick was a coin club "regular" when he worked at the mines in Chibougamau. When next I met him, it was in New Brunswick, an active "coin" person with the splendid Miramichi group. Then, Northern Ontario — Jim's country — I've been told. Mining people and their families do get around, but such an interest as coin collecting does travel well. A most interesting preoccupation, all in all!

His "papers" Jim turned over to me for the purposes of this project ... and what a treasure trove of memorabilia and source items! Jim's *Coin World* columns on Canadian numismatic "trends" (see Section 4). These would be crumbling after three and more decades, of course, had not Jim had the foresight to photocopy on better paper. Rough notes for talks at clubs. Write-ups from club bulletins. Numismatic bits and pieces from a Canadian Press clipping service. A wealth of meticulous manuscript material, much of it penned for these efforts. Catalogues galore. Plus hundreds of photographs that span eight decades and show Jim's life and hint at why he is all that he is.

In assembling this wealth of source material, our priority has been to present Jim, the person, in the context of those around him and the interests and activities that have sustained him. You'll see Jim in his childhood in The Beaches, in East End Toronto. This period is rich in nostalgia. You'll see him working through the Depression, then finding great opportunity in Northern Ontario. We've photos of Jim in Militia uniform, and in the uniform of a Salvation Army corps sergeant-major. Jim will tell you of war years in a northern munition plant, and a subsequent relocation to a new facility, of initially undisclosed purpose, up at Chalk River.

Then Toronto and the *Toronto Star*, as the coin business boomed — though, as you read between the lines, this is more than the classic "being in the right place at the right time." Jim and his catalogues helped to forge the place and the time.

We live all too much in a world of pieces of paper, and much such documentation Jim has shared for this project. His Royal Numismatic Society (London) fellowship, a status that he maintained throughout his working years. His

Canadian Numismatic Association "J. Douglas Ferguson Award" citation. Honorary memberships, in national groups and in grateful local clubs. Documentation of five golfing "holes in one." Yet the paper that he values most highly is his First Class credential as Stationary Engineer. He well knows the effort that goes into such attainment. And at one point he wonders whether perhaps there shouldn't be more rigour along the path to numismatic professionalism.

Should you be looking for advice as to how to achieve wealth through the coin hobby, Jim might suggest that you emulate his lifelong friend John Jay Pittman, who certainly did — and had a great time doing it. Seek out quality material, the very best — and hold it for a long time. Jim has a fat file relating to others' excesses — the rolls and mint bags and coin sets of the Sixties. He has filed buy-back offers and lavish promises alongside bankruptcy papers from when the "bubble" inevitably burst.

Jim, let it be said, is a most able writer, a meticulous craftsman with words. One of the better things that Jim has done, I think, is an overview of Canadian monetary history, "O Canada: Wampum to Tokens, Beavers to Loons," run as a World Coins supplement to *Coin World*, the weekly newspaper, back in January 1988 (see Bibliography, Reference 35).

A delightful blend of Oriental insight and of timeless wisdom, I sense implicit in that ancient Chinese wish (or was it curse?), "May you live in interesting times."

To a lengthy succession of undeniably "interesting times," Jim Charlton will be seen to have responded distinctly well: the Great Depression (honest hard work, wherever it could be found), the War Years (strategic industries, northern smelters, Chalk River), the post-War boom (Toronto, with markedly increased responsibility), then "coin" activities that were to expand beyond anyone's wildest dreams. Two strong decades of numismatic — and business — growth and development. Then a long planned for, frequently interrupted, "early retirement" — all of 30 years ago. Followed by a unique and distinguished contribution as role model and elder statesman to "numismatic Canada" — science, intellectual interest, hobby, and profession.

Quite apart from his pioneering catalogue preparation and development in the coin, token, and paper money fields,

Jim's related efforts in numismatic journalism brought him into extended contact with "interesting times."

With the fascination of a long-time auctioneer, dealer, cataloguer — and collector — Jim continued to monitor the "progress" of Canada's three "glamour coins," the 1921 silver 5¢, the 1921 silver 50¢ (both of which had, in the main, achieved "rarity" by being relegated to the melting pots), and the country's 1911 "pattern" silver dollar (References 82, 83). He also recognized great interest in our 1889 10¢, whose rarity long was underappreciated. Canada's famed "dot" coinage (1936-dated) I find less reference to in Jim's files, though it has commanded impressive prices. It brings back my boyhood memory of finding two "dot" coins in circulation within a week — needless to say, both 25¢ pieces, and so worn that identification was more by the dot than by the date!

Jim's "papers" — voluminous gatherings of written source materials, plus a wealth of things photographic — have been accessible to me in assembling these "reflections," as has continuing opportunity for written and spoken dialogue. His wide interests encompassed Canadian and world numismatics crossing through all phases of coin, token, and paper money, even into the numismatic industry and the press that it supports. During his business years, Jim subscribed to a national clipping service, and much that he received in this manner is intriguing. As well, Jim received a great range of "coin" papers, *Numismatic News*, *Coin World*, Hewitt Brothers' *Numismatic Scrapbook Magazine*, and such Canadian ventures as *Coin, Stamp Antique News*, *Canada Coin News*, and the present-day *Canadian Coin News*. Leafing through such papers, I see Jim appearing on Canadian television in support of National Coin Week — front page centre in *The Coin Collector*, "The World's Greatest Paper for Coin and Stamp Collectors," Anamosa, Iowa, 20 April 1958. Jim's "archives" also reveal carefully preserved copies of such as Jack Veffer's ambitious (though short-lived) *Numismatic Courier*, and Paul Nadin-Davis' *Canadian Numismatist*, later *Canadian Numismatic Quarterly*.

"This was a big help to me and many others," Jim has endorsed on the plastic that serves to preserve a much-handled and crumbling brochure that is the forerunner of Jim's long-term cataloguing effort. Its title and subtitle say it well: *The Coins and Tokens of Canada*. An illustrated list of all the types of Canadian Coins and Tokens from 1670 to date, including the official mint reports from 1858 to 1946. The Coin Collector Series, Number 12. New York: Wayte Ramond, Inc., 1947. Pp. 32. Interesting browsing. Well, not all rarities receive immediate recognition: Canada's 1921 50¢ was priced at $2.00 Fine, $3.00 Uncirculated (compare with $10.00 and $17.00 for the 1932), but a 1921 silver 5¢ already was $25.00 Fine, $40.00 Uncirculated.

Some of the most intriguing of Jim's memorabilia all but defies classification, but is none the less worth sharing. One document, a mere carbon copy, which Jim has carefully preserved, comprises childhood recollections of a man I well remember, Allan Fargeon, a Montreal Coin Club stalwart of the late Fifties. Jim no doubt saved it because he knew Fargeon, an affable and serious collector, and knew the period being described. I find it most interesting because it was a decade before my time.

"My interest in coins," Fargeon recalls, "began when I was about four years of age. One indelible incident which was responsible for creating this interest occurred when our neighbourhood Chinese laundry handed us in change, together with other large cents circulating then, two 1852 Quebec Papineau half-pennies."

Fargeon speaks of "copper" coins of three reigns, English pennies and half-pennies, and occasional New Brunswick silver coins.

"One summer day, later in the Twenties, I recall my curiosity at a New Brunswick half-penny that was showing on a tray mixed with all kinds of foreign pieces, for sale in a small upholstery store which sold antiques as well, located on Montreal's "Main Street," St. Lawrence Boulevard. This I could not resist, and paid out a quarter for. As I write this, a third of a century later, it is still worth only a quarter."

Fargeon laments that in Montreal in the Twenties there was no dealer or fellow-collector to whom a "wide-eyed brat" could turn.

"In the early Thirties, I visited the Chateau de Ramsay, as I enjoyed heading downtown to the old and historic section of Montreal. There, on many a Saturday afternoon, I would meet with the revered curator at that time, Mr. L. A. Renaud, with whom a friendship and an affection mutually existed until his last days. This Dean of Canadian Numismatics one can never forget, was the link between the Golden Age of our early numismatic history and the legacy which he left for us today. It was poignant to hear him recall his youth when his mentor and ideal had been one of the Fathers of Canadian Numismatics, Mr. Adelard Boucher, then of quite advanced age."

I recall my own one meeting with Mr. Renaud when I was in the summer employ of another museum. I can understand how Allan Fargeon must have felt.

I have suggested to Jim that such papers as these be entrusted some day to a provincial or national archive, or to such an institution as the A.N.A., where they can be properly kept for generations of collectors as yet unborn.

A rather remarkable brochure and "order form" preserved in Jim's papers had me more than ready to reach for postage stamp and cheque book — $3! — if only today's Postal Service could transport a letter half a century and more, backward in time. With fellow-Ontarian William H. Kernohan's pioneer efforts in visual numismatics, Jim evidently had been well impressed, and understandably so. Kernohan's unique "labour of love" had been a pair of remarkable wall hangings, "The History of Canada in Money," covering intervals 1534-1866 and 1866-1945. The oversize, lavishly illustrated charts had been intended primarily for children and the classroom — in the conviction, not unreasonable, that youngsters could soon be interested in Canada's money, and Canada's history — through such a well-considered visual presentation. Through wampum, "international" coinage, tokens, and crude, early paper (the first interval) to familiar Canadian "type coins" and diverse folding money — shinplaster and $4, $25, and $500 legal tender bills, in colour, and some chartered bank classics — over 20 gorgeous notes in all. Kernohan is known to have fought a protracted running battle with officialdom (personified by former note signer W. C. Clark) — to be tolerated, were permission as such deemed impossible, in his well-intentioned educational venture.

When recently, to my pleasant surprise, I chanced upon a carefully preserved set of Kernohan Charts in a place of honour, the setting was the distinguished old Dominion

Bank head office building, where Toronto-Dominion Bank archives were being maintained.

An ironic touch is that while Kernohan had had great commitment to collecting and sharing such visual history, he himself had been totally blind.

Reports the brochure: "At present, Mr. Kernohan is sending copies of the charts to Boards of Education throughout the country, and he has received many favourable comments. He hopes that before long they will be hanging in school rooms from Victoria to Charlottetown."

That quotation originally derives from the Spring 1948 issue of *National News of the Blind.*

Jim now tells me that, unlike James Elliott, his predecessor in attempted cataloguing of "Canadian paper," he had opted to go for illustrations form the beginning, taking the Kernohan precedent as an indication that such might be done.

So, you have the story of these remarkable visuals, and now you know where a set still may be seen.

Also accessible will be full-page illustrations of both charts, reproduced shortly after Kernohan's death, in the *Canadian Numismatic Journal,* November 1965, pp. 450, 452.

Jim's first interval as *Coin World* "Trends" columnist (7 July 1961 to 1 October 1969) was highlighted, at its start, by unprecedented "growth" in the coin hobby, a less-than-healthy growth characterized by intense, often ill-advised "coin" speculation (rolls and bags of recent, common coins, References 13, 95), and the soon-to-burst bubble of Canadian "proof-like set" speculative investment (Reference 31, 80, 100). The "bubble" burst, as burst it had to, when Canadian finance minister Walter Gordon announced that all orders for the then-current 1965-dated sets, at that point being quoted by dealers at $12 to $14 a set, would be filled, at the Mint's prevailing $4 price (Reference 80).

"Interesting times!"

Jim recalls for us how he was flown to the U.S. to address a university extension course on such investment. He had counseled the group that any numismatic investing be conservative, involving long-term commitment to quality items — a view that he retains to this day, making reference to such life-long collectors as his friend of some decades, John Jay Pittman.

Technology can change our world, shift our perspective, even we coin collectors — then rapidly deteriorate in its own unplanned obsolescence. Those clattering teletype machines that dominated much of numismatic merchandising in the speculative Sixties are all but forgotten (References 86, 94). I do, however, recall an upscale California outlet where the proprietor had been loath to glance up from the machine when I had ventured into his retail store. Jim retained a directory of the then-active Canadian circuit, and the businesses and individual names recalled in Appendix I, do evoke memories.

Canada's 1967-dated "Centennial" coinage, the first of several ventures in innovative designs and inscriptions for circulation coinage (the 1992 "double dates," the turn-of-millennium 25¢ pieces), was not without controversy. The asking price of $40 for $21.91 face value (including the $20 gold) was questioned (Reference 19). The coinage designs themselves aroused mixed feelings, especially when some of the "also rans" were shared with numismatic readers. Or so Jim's clippings document rather well.

Now, animal likenesses on the six accepted designs were highly skilled, and quite attractive — as one would expect in the work of a leading art professional. Some of the runners up, however, showed distinct strength in what I would term "coinage design" in itself. Some feeling for this I developed through service on six Royal Canadian Mint selection committees, if only for non-circulating "collector" silver and gold. On those occasions, imaginative designs, having real eye appeal, seemed conceived for murals, wall hangings, or dinner plates, not for something as small and constrained as a coin. On one occasion — the Olympic gold, as I recall — our committee voted to reject all submissions, to reopen the competition — and we got our way. Coin papers allowed readers to view, and to respond to, unaccepted Centennial designs (References 42, 61, 62). I have Jim's marginal notation that it was through his efforts that the information had been released.

Even, perhaps especially, in retirement, Jim has taken on commitments that were demanding and diverse. His records reflect this. He was involved, as a government witness, in Tax Court of Canada deliberations, 1984-1986, relating to valuation of groups of numismatic items donated to a Canadian museum (References 51, 76). The trial and its outcome received significant coverage in the numismatic press (References 2, 21, 52, 78).

Jim's "papers," I find, include unique material of considerable fascination. One item so perceived by both Jim and me is a remarkable, *eight-sheet*, meticulously penned listing of note hoards known to him in, very possibly, the late Fifties. Included are no less than 78 of the Prince of Wales (later Edward VII) $2 Dominion of Canada notes of 1897. Jim tells me that he wasn't successful in obtaining this hoard, but that the dealer who did was obliging in sharing his records. And Jim retained them. Sheet numbers and position letters had been meticulously recorded, from such as 059829/C ("red back") to 999195/C. In numerical order. Quite a tally. Complete with position letters, an essential component in identification of a particular note. (Dealers who should know better — 40 years later — may omit position letters when citing "serial (sheet) numbers" in "for sale" advertisements to this day.) Then, alas, I did a double take! Three components, not two, are essential to identify uniquely a Dominion of Canada 1897 $2 bill: the series letter (or absence of such), sheet number, and position letter. Jim's people, back then, had identified two out of three. Current cataloguers, in their wisdom, depict only the pricey, low-number "reddish-brown back," which has no series letter and therefore gives no indication where such a designation is placed. "Series A," for a sheet in the second million, through "Series I," for the uncompleted tenth million, appears (on back plate) in the signature panel, dead centre. Indeed, Mr. (or Ms.) MacArthur, in hand-signing my "Series H" $2, had to bend the last part of the signature to avoid covering the series designation. So that $2 hoard, like its $1 companion listing, is of much interest, but of diminished value because of the missing "serial number" component.

One really can't fault Jim's colleague of decades ago for his omission. The knowledge of what to watch for simply wasn't accessible. It would be quite a different matter today.

From an accompanying list of chartered bank serial numbers, these fully recorded, one particularly fascinating group — its appearance suggests a pioneer mini-collection — consists of "domiciled" Bank of Toronto $5 and $10 notes, from back when the overprinting of the branch name was standard practice at that important bank. All of these notes, no doubt, survive in collections, and their present owners may be interested that it was Jim Charlton who saved their notes from the furnace.

Bank of Toronto $5 notes, issue of 1 January 1890: 170250/E on Peterboro, 186812/C on London, 249532/E on Montreal, 255814/E on Creemore, 277767/D on Winnipeg, 292123/E on Point St. Charles (a Montreal neighbourhood), 300608/D on Coldwater, 327436/B on Niagara Falls Centre, 349770/C on Point St. Charles, 350779/C on Victoria Harbour.

Bank of Toronto $5 notes, issue of 1 February 1906: 314280/D on Gaspe, 325627 on St. Catharines, 374547 on Waterloo, and higher numbers, evidently undomiciled, 486618/C and 669800/B.

Bank of Toronto $10 note, issue of 1 June 1892: 040803/D on London.

Jim, as businessman, coin dealer and collector, has had and has shown great interest in standards for coin grading, particularly as they relate to Canadian decimal series: The reference work which he co-authored with Bob Willey stands as testimony to this long-term commitment (Reference 36).

The *Canadian Numismatic Journal,* "from 1956 to 1965 was the sole outlet for numismatic articles generated by the membership," long-time member Ross W. Irwin observed in a "letter" published in the *Journal* for July/August 2000. Irwin recalls that a certain numismatic orthodoxy (my term) in article acceptance had been a factor contributing to the formation of such "splinter groups" as the Canadian Association of Token Collectors and the Canadian Paper Money Society. Quite possibly. I remember having had an early paper money article turned down by the *Journal* with a criticism of its terminology. Fair enough. I had, however, spent time in American Bank Note Company executive offices on New York's Broad Street, and terms were correct for the industry, if not yet for the hobby. No problem, though. I took the rejected article which I'd been prepared to give to the C.N.A, sent it off to Lee Hewitt's *Numismatic Scrapbook Magazine* in Chicago, and used the generous cheque to pay dealer Phil Spier for my Weyburn Security Bank $5, which still gives me much pleasure. However, each in his own way, Jim and I found ways to publish. When the Montreal Coin Club, in 1960, compiled 40 of my articles in booklet form (Reference 4), acknowledged sources included: two A.N.A. convention papers, 11 articles from Bill and Chris Johns' *Coins Unlimited* (published in Texas), five articles from Frank Spadone's *Flying Eaglet* (published in New Jersey), four from Chet Krause's *Numismatic News*, two from *Numismatic Scrapbook*, and five from Canadian weeklies. *Coin World*, which Jim was to serve so well, had only arrived on the scene.

International writing still challenges me, and I'm pleased when I'm translated, as into Dutch (Reference 7), or receive follow-up letters from a country that I first must locate on the map.

"Whereas Toronto is now being considered the coin capital of Canada..." Donald D. Summerville, then Toronto mayor, is prominently featured in the Canadian Section — Jim's section — of the *Coin World* issue of 28 June 1963, used those words in proclaiming a coin and stamp event. To a yet earlier generation, that "capital" likely would have been Montreal. Jim urges that we not overlook vigorous numismatic activity in Atlantic Canada, in Quebec, across the Prairies, and in British Columbia. Also, there are fine people, coast to coast, who don't fit into the neat slots of topics due for consideration. They are not forgotten. I sense what Jim means. Recently, being in Montreal on the right evening, I looked in at the Montreal Numismatic Society (Montreal Coin Club), for the first time in 40 years! Familiar faces? Ocatvio Butcher, career broadcaster on Radio Canada's Brazilian Service, was first to greet me. He had brought with him the *Canadian Numismatic Journal* for April 1959, the issue which I had guest edited. Featured had been his illustrated article, "How Interesting is Brazilian Coinage?" Such 40-year collectors with specialized interests do have much to share. My own 18 years in Atlantic Canada gave me additional perspective on organized Canadian numismatics. The fine folks at the Halifax Coin Club were more than worth the logistics of an occasional overnight trip, I always felt much "at home" at Newcastle events, that wonderful New Brunswick area serving to recall my woodsy Chibougamau days. So I much appreciate Jim's Central Canada focus, and share his concern that, in these reflections, none has reason to feel "left out."

To me, the really fine people in organized numismatics are typified by Jim ... and by Bernie Kline and his delightful Aunt Edna, the most reliable of Halifax — and Atlantic Provinces — attendees. Collectors from the Miramichi and east should know whereof I write!

Allow me, if you will, to tender an unsolicited, but considered, testimonial for the Canadian Numismatic Association and Numismatic Educational Services Association *Canadian Numismatic Correspondence Course* St. Eligius Press, 1966). I "took" the course several years ago — to test it — and was indeed impressed. You see, I very well know that a singularly tough job in education is to prepare material from which others will teach (or self-teach), and learn. Such "adult education" material, in my academic field, I have been contracted to produce in two Canadian jurisdictions, Nova Scotia and the Eastern Arctic (Baffin Region) — believe me, it can be a demanding and humbling experience, even after 43 classroom years. So, it is with some feeling that I strongly commend C.N.A. efforts. I similarly "took" A.N.A.'s Young Numismatist course some years previously — which was sound. My reservation was and is use of "young" rather than, say, "new." It would seem to imply an attitude, an approach. Youngsters don't much like being "talked down to," if the alternative can be being expected to, and assisted in, appropriately measuring up.

In numismatic matters as otherwise, Jim indeed has witnessed times of change. When Robert Obojski reported in "Auction Scene" (*Canadian Coin News*, 23 May 1995): "An English language format $500 Canadian note of 1935 ... in VF to EF was hammered down for $9,075 at Bowers and Merena Galleries sale of the Herman Halpern Collection," Jim noted marginally, "I couldn't sell three at $515 each." His three $500's he used at his printer's toward catalogue printing costs, "way back when." Judging by the flash of rose pink and reddish purple on today's bourse floors — those last two releases of Bank of Canada $1000's — high face values don't intimidate prospective buyers, at least not to the extent that they once did.

Jim, his catalogues, his sales and auctions, did much to bring Canadian coin series to the attention of United States collectors. What he has had to say about this is interesting. I find in it considerable food for thought.

"Americans, in some ways, differ fundamentally from their British and European counterparts. In the old countries, numismatics, as such, is a long established science and pursuit. Chief interest, it would seem, has lain among the professional and well educated classes. As a consequence, the study and collecting of ancient coins long has been popular. A strong background in ancient history and a working knowledge of Greek and Latin are most helpful for investigation and interpretation of Greek and Roman coins. In the United States — and Canada — coin collecting is more widely spread through the ranks. The bulk of present-day American coin collectors, lacking the training to enter readily into classical numismatics and finding less appeal in modern foreign coins, have become collectors of American coins, most often recent and more accessible issues. Compared with, say, British, American coins, and equally so Canadian, span a relatively short interval, and the North American collectors has been less satisfied by "type coins" than, say, his United Kingdom counterpart. He has turned to collecting by dates.

"After World War II, many American collectors found their series near complete, except for rarities that they could ill afford. They looked around for a possible new field. The long neglected Canadian series seemed made to order for them. Once dated, priced catalogues existed, the series took off."

My source here is interesting. It is Jim's unpublished, handwritten notes for a paper at the Metropolitan Washington Numismatic Association Educational Forum, back in July 1978.

"The '1913' Nickel of Canada: First Time Offered at Auction on This Continent." That heading from the 1948 A.N.A. Convention Auction, Sale No. 8 of Frank H. Katen's Milford Coin & Stamp Company, New Haven, might well have caused you to do a double take, but read on.

The 1913 Liberty Head 5¢ is, of course, a classic United States rarity. But, "1913 Nickel of Canada"? The coin being compared is Canada's 1921 silver 5¢, for which the auctioneer was trying to suggest a value.

"Although the mint reports show a total of 2,501,238 pieces, only 8 or 10 are actually known. What became of the balance is mere conjecture."

Suggested value?

"We shall not hazard a guess on what this piece will bring but will rely on the auction bids for it to find its level, be it $100 or $1,000."

The offered coin had "seen considerable wear but very easily graded better than very good."

The prices realized?

In Jim's papers is Katen's letter to the Canadian consignor, Norman B. Mason of Toronto: "Enclosed please find my check for $21.60 in full settlement": that is, $27.00 (the winning bid), less a commission of 20 per cent."

One fact seemed to make the auctioneer a bit uncomfortable, however: the 5¢ coin was cataloguing at twelve times the price of the corresponding Canadian "half dollar," "despite the recent statements made by Mr. J. Douglas Ferguson that he knows of only four half dollar pieces as against three times that number of five cent pieces."

Knowledge that we take for granted today — see your latest Charlton catalogue — was not all that readily amassed!

Back when I was 10 or 12 years old, I had two "twins" — both girls. I got both the way Canadian youngsters got twins in those pre-cloning days — through well-read columns of *The Family Herald and Weekly Star*. You turned to children's pages, sought names with your exact birth date, and approached them to be "pen pals." Both my "twins" were farm girls, one in Manitoba, the other in an Ontario location that I couldn't find on the map, "Chalk River."

It's a world of coincidence. Jim was to be power house chief engineer, when Chalk River (the plant) and Deep River (the new residential area) ushered Canada into the Atomic Age. And the *Family Herald*? Well, they're the family values farm paper that declined to run a "coin" ad sent in by Jim.

Reader complaints about such ads — and such advertisers — had led to the policy decision not to accept coin dealer advertising. Jim had been informed.

I suspect that that had made Jim think!

Now, the North American newspaper of choice in our family today is *The New York Times*, particularly those hefty Sunday issues with magazine sections. Especially thought-provoking for me is a weekly column, Randy Cohen's "The Ethicist," which poses and seeks to resolve reader-submitted ethical dilemmas. Clearly, such matters all too seldom come in black or white.

Jim took a strong stand on a numismatic point with deeper ethical implications, some years back, voicing well-considered views on bourse floor "cherrypicking" (Reference 34). Is a customer ever entitled to take advantage of superior knowledge to buy a coin for substantially less that he knows it to be worth? *Coin World* raised —and considered —this basic question (References 39, 54, 57). Jim's response gives provocative food for thought. *The Canadian Numismatic Journal* could do worse than to feature regular dialogue on "coin ethics." I can even suggest who a great moderator would be.

Such ethical dilemmas, you sense, would seem to be surprisingly common in popular numismatics. I vividly recall one relevant incident, fairly far from home. In a bedroom community within the urban sprawl south of Los Angeles, a colleague with whom I'd spent a summer up at Santa Clara had invited me to spend a day with his family on my detour south to Mexican Border numismatics. For the evening, knowing my interests, he had taken me to the local coin club. A significant focus had been an acquisitive sort of show and tell. A speaker had shown his new coin, and had narrated how he'd gotten it — a real bargain — from a friend. The audience had been distinctly approving. Shortchanging a friend! — my colleague later had confided to me that he couldn't remember having been more embarrassed than by that disclosure and the collective response.

Jim, on reading these pages, clearly was moved to reflection — in his case, from a dealer perspective. Reflection was followed by dialogue, and he invited the thoughts of Dan Gosling, the collector with the greatest evidenced interest in "Charlton" catalogues and business commitments. Gosling's response was detailed and thought provoking. At one point he said in effect:

"Sellers are naturally suspicious when trying to dispose of their holdings. They want to know if they are being cheated. If they are not comfortable with the amount being offered, it might be best to suggest that they not sell. Indicating the resale value can generate confidence. Separating the pile into common, bullion and collector groupings can assist the seller in understanding the dealer's offer."

The lot of the "coin" professional is not an easy one, I am the first to acknowledge. Gosling writes:

"While dealers clearly must generate a profit, they have an ethical obligation to purchase at a fair value. Dealers are in a position of trust in the community, and must protect the general public from being 'ripped off.'"

A "Dealers Code of Ethics," above and beyond a "Members Code of Ethics," the highly influential American Numismatic Association has approved (August 1967) and revised (February 1995). Gosling provided both a copy and the web site:

http://anamarket.money.org/EthicsCode.html

Any teeth to it?

The "bottom line" should be indicative: "Any violation of this code will be grounds for expulsion from the American Numismatic Association."

I recently navigated the potentially treacherous shoals of South East Asian business and commerce, my sole travel guide an A.N.A. list of relevant member dealers. In such cities as Singapore and Kuala Lumpur, I was most hospitably received by world-class dealers, justifiably proud of their long-term A.N.A. affiliation, and responsive to the numismatic heritage that we shared.

Coin World, as you perhaps know, has been rigorously "policing" its advertisers for 40 years.

Through my term of office as International Bank Note Society president — early in the organization's history — ethical differences, on a world scale, between member and member, or member and dealer, were among the toughest problems that we sought to resolve.

Always will be, I suspect. But putting the spotlight on such differences and their hobby implications may be one of the more important things that we should to do.

Formalizing "ethics" into the deliberations and decisions of courts of law, Jim's files attest to deep interest in court cases which touch on numismatics, in particular in two cases in which he was called as an expert witness. One was a tax court case with, observers have suggested, significant possible hobby implications (References 51, 76; then 2, 52, 78). The other was the "Chameau treasure" court actions. Of the later, Jim gives some particulars in these pages, and a quite detailed record in an accessible source (Reference 32).

Jim's "papers" also attest to great interest in Sixties excesses, where so many were left poorer but wiser after rampant "proof-like" and bulk coin speculation (see, especially, References 13, 31).

All too often, at least in the public eye, it's big-ticket numismatic items that make headlines — the "prince," "king," "emperor" and such, of Canadian coins, though none of those, in truth, much entered into Canadian circulation. I find it interesting what some in the hobby actually collect. Doug Ferguson collected everything, though he once acknowledged that he found dated sequences Canada's "least interesting" realm. Al Bliman — so active with C.A.N.D., C.N.A., and C.P.M.S. — "collected everything from coins to spoons to woods to paper money," Jim has communicated to me, Bliman's "passion" in later years having been casino chips. (Having more than once almost missed a Greyhound bus by hunting such chips in some one-horse Nevada town, I can identify with that!) Jim himself collected "odd and curious," an open field in which he felt comfortable that he and his clients wouldn't be in conflict. Far out! I don't know a group in (or adjacent to) this country's numismatics getting more pleasure than Canadian Tire "coupon" collectors, though even there, "investment" is mentioned, and auction prices on rare varieties are moving sharply upward.

"Bubble gum cards," an older generation will assure you, were the true forerunners of today's collectable sports cards, and came in considerable diversity. My recollection is that, with the War, "license plate" gum cards of 1939 gave way to "Aviation," "Marine," and "Victory" series — the latter favouring such as tanks and antiaircraft guns. Some such cards survive in nostalgia shops. I wonder whether any of Jim's postwar "coin cards" also might be found.

"Coin Cards — an easy reference to fun and profit," Jim's cards were enclosures in packages of Lever Potato Chips, produced in St. Catharines, Ontario. Each card was black on deep orange, 57 mm by 83 mm, pictured a numismatic collectable, usually obverse and reverse, and stated an approximate valuation: "Authority Canada Coin Exchange," with the Richmond Street business address. The back of the card related the item's collector interest, articulately and in some detail. Thus Card 56 depicted Canada's 1870-dated 25 cent note, "Approx. Value $3.00," and informed the reader:

"Canadian 25¢ fractional currency commonly called shinplasters were issued dated 1870, 1900 and 1923. More than 5 million of these small bills were in circulation in 1929 but since then the number has steadily declined. In 1935 the Bank of Canada ordered that they be recalled from circulation so they are now seldom seen. The expression shinplaster is attributed to the use of similar bills by soldiers of the Revolutionary War period as a lining to prevent their shins chafing."

Some other cards that Jim still has among his papers tell of the 1858 Canadian 20¢ piece ($20.00), 1907H large cent ($4.50), 1930 Canadian cent (75¢), 1935 Canadian $25.00 bill ($70.00) and 1942 "brass" 5¢ piece (75¢). Jim informs me that he did have some customer response, primarily for the like of the 1948 10¢ piece ($2.00 approximate value), and that cheques had been sent to such finders.

Jim especially recalls several numismatic commitments that fell outside his normal range of business and "hobby" activities. One was attendance and participation in the Fifteenth General Assembly of the International Association of Professional Numismatists, held in 1966 in New York City. This was Jim's initial experience with U.N.-style multilingual simultaneous translation. Jim also had a say in design selection for four recent Canadian coin releases. Serving by invitation on Royal Canadian Mint selection committees, he helped to choose, from submitted art, the designs for: 1978 Commonwealth Games, Edmonton, silver dollar (Raymond Taylor, designer); 1979 International Year of the Child $100 gold coin (Carola Tietz); 1990 Henry Kelsey Tricentennial silver dollar (John Mardon); and 1990

International Literacy Year $100 gold coin (Dora de Pédery-Hunt).

"A good friend for nearly 50 years," Jim penned in the margin of the John J. Pittman obituary, as it appeared in *Canadian Coin News* of 9 April 1996. Obituaries tend to be mainly factual, perhaps necessarily so. Those who knew Pittman as A.N.A. and C.N.A. president, as a collector's collector, and exhibitor *extraordinaire* will want to seek a companion document penned by Polly, Pittman's daughter (*Coin World*, 8 September 1997, pp. 84-94). "Contrary to what many people think, John Jay Pittman did not come from money. He was the oldest of seven children and was 10 years old before he had a new pair of shoes." I can understand why Jim Charlton has that in his file of clippings about friends. They don't write leads like that any more.

About Jim ...

The Numismatic Literary Guild, whose members tend to have a way with words, referred to Jim in its *Numismatic Newsletter* (July 1968) as 'one of the guiding forces of the Canadian numismatic world."

Somewhat more thought provoking, at least to Jim, was this line from the Bowers and Merena auction catalogue of the Norwood Collection, 15 November 1996:

"The late Jim Charlton was the foremost dealer exponent of Canadian numismatics in the early 1950s and left a rich trail of accomplishments."

Jim chuckles that "the late" had merited a letter of apology from a foremost cataloguer. But he had welcomed the compliment that the remark had implied.

When Jim first invited me to take on this project, I promptly approached, through coin papers and at meetings, those who had known Jim, to share anecdotes and insights that would serve to introduce Jim, and would put his good works in proper perspective. I want to share five such communications — from Wm. Waychison, Gerald L. Kochel, Chet Krause, Terry A. Campbell, Harry Eisenhauer, and Philip J. Carrigan — then to join Ray Mah of North Vancouver in an additional insight which he and I thought to be particularly significant.

Each in turn:

Wm. Waychison of Timmins, Ontario, writes that his retained interest in numismatics as a student is directly attributable to Jim's 1964 edition, which he bought at Spiers' in Montreal. "As a student I could not afford most of the coins in the catalogue, even at their then low price. I had been collecting slowly for a few years, but it was the book and the images, always available, that maintained and fueled my interest." The old, worn catalogue "still has a place on my shelf."

Many of us can identify with that.

Care for an anecdote that would seem to set matters in proper perspective? Gerald L. Kochel has written from Lititz, Pennsylvania, with a tale that dates back to the American Numismatic Association convention in Miami in 1974.

I'll let him tell his story:

"I love to exhibit, and have done so for the past 27 A.N.A. conventions. Early on during my exhibiting jaunts I had an exhibit entitled 'Canada's Victory Nickel.' It was a small one-case exhibit, with four coins worth, in aggregate, about $3.00. However, I did have beautiful artwork, and an 8" x 10" photograph of the coin's reverse, pointing out the Morse code, 'We Win When We Work Willingly.'

"The exhibit placed second in its category, 'Canadian Coins.' I had proven that one does not need a lot of money or high-powered numismatic items to win an award, even at national level.

"But, to my displeasure, my critics — my fellow exhibitors — set out to prove me wrong.

"At the Judging and Exhibiting Seminar, critics proceeded to down-grade my exhibit. 'It's not a good enough exhibit to win a Second, because coins aren't worth much,' one said. Another asserted that there weren't enough coins in the exhibit, possibly not realizing that the 'Victory' piece was a war issue struck for only three consecutive years (1943, 1944, 1945).

"During the height of the criticism, none other than 'Mr. Canadian Numismatics' — Jim Charlton — entered the room. Immediately, the seminar moderator addressed the question to Jim: 'Mr. Charlton, what did you think of the one-case Canadian Victory nickel exhibit?' Jim replied: 'I did not judge the exhibit, but if I had I would have rated it higher.'

"Well, my 'critics' retreated in a hurry, and the meeting moved on to another topic.

"I later thanked Jim for his comments. I've always respected him as the authority on Canadian coins.

"At subsequent conventions, I made a point to greet Jim, and to talk to him about our favourite hobby."

Well said.

It's a small world, Jerry. I also was in that room, and to the best of my recollection was one of your judges. I know I liked the exhibit, and what, to me, it represented.

A most interesting letter, just received, from Krause Publications, publishers of *Numismatic News* and of so much more, admirably serves to move these "perspectives" toward an apt conclusion. I have written in *Numismatic News*, off and on, since the Fifties, and have been most hospitably received by Chet Krause and staff (see Reference 71 for a recent update on the extraordinary corporate history) — so a letter from Chet Krause, the founder, was most welcome.

Here's what Chet had to contribute:

"When I first hit the numismatic trail there were two men I admired greatly, Jim Charlton and Dick Yeoman. Both were of high personal character as well as highly knowledgeable in their field. They were the men who put coin collecting on the map in Canada and the United States, and to the best of my ability I've tried to perpetuate their dream."

Elsewhere, Chet had spoke of Jim as "one of those outstanding examples of what this hobby community should be all about" (letter, 30 June 1998). He had added, "I remember well purchasing and enjoying early editions of the Charlton catalogue, back when I was a fledgling collector."

Acknowledging Jim's generous support for his "Dear Abby of Canadian Numismatics" role as *Canadian Coin News*

"Questions and Answers" columnist, Terry A Campbell of Oshawa, Ontario, has shared with us the following insight:

"While attending an Ontario Numismatic Association convention in Toronto several years ago, I was approached by a number of junior numismatists from Chris Boyer's Taylor Evans Public School, who asked me to autograph O.N.A. programs for them.

"I had been to their school the previous year, and had spoken to this group, and also had shown them a slide program on error coins. I'd also given a talk at the Kitchener/Waterloo Coin Club, on which occasion a number of these youngsters had been present. I complied with their request to sign programs.

"Jim Charlton was standing at a neighbouring dealer's table, talking with people there. I suggested to the autograph hunters that they get the Charlton signature. They asked "Who's he?" Well, after giving a brief verbal biography, to convince them that indeed they should seek his autograph, they somewhat reluctantly followed me across the aisleway.

"On being introduced to Jim, they cautiously asked him to sign programs. This he did, on an individual basis, speaking with each briefly before resuming his conversation with the dealer. Jim seemed a little surprised by his sudden celebrity status, but handled it like the gentleman that he is. The balance of the group's cronies, for the rest of the day, frequented Jim, as they sought his John Hancock."

Harry Eisenhauer, one of those whose numismatic life and love has been Canadian paper, articulately acknowledges a twofold debt to Jim. First, he writes, to Jim as mentor, helping and supporting him in person and through extended correspondence, as Harry laboured with note registers and sought the questions that, in due course, would lead to useful answers and insights. Further, Harry points out a second indebtedness to Jim, one that we all share. Jim's prodigious efforts to rescue notes from "the firey furnace" — his phrasing — back when this could be done, have direct implications for what now exists for us to study and to collect. Harry writes:

"I ask all collectors of Canadian paper money to take the necessary time to do research and to track down where some of their great Canadian notes originated from, years ago. I believe that they will find that, somewhere in the past, Jim possessed those notes. He rescued them, and as a consequence they may be enjoyed by present and future collectors. We owe Jim a serious vote of appreciation for that important deed."

Yet another letter:

"I knew the name Charlton for 30 years, as a young collector of Canadian coins where these appeared in change in Massachusetts." So writes Philip J. Carrigan, an A.N.A. and C.N.A. life member residing in Round Lake, Illinois. "This limited and distant knowledge existed with the seeing of a photo of Jim now and again in a *Canadian Numismatic Journal.* The latter proved he was alive and well."

Then, our correspondent took the logical next step:

"A few years ago, I decided to write to Jim and to ask a question about his auction sales, conducted in the 1950s and 1960s. What a wonderful move on my part! I discovered a splendid numismatic friend who provides thoughts and insights from the past and who comments on the present scene. Jim is an astute and keen observer of events both before and now."

Also, field work. Near the start of this project, our daughter, who was living there, escorted me to a church hall in North Vancouver, British Columbia, for an advertised meeting of the community numismatic group. Actually, I was literally on my way to Vancouver International Airport, for an overnight flight east; but I wanted to ask these folks for recollections of Jim. Their response to the word "Charlton" was "catalogue" and not "Jim," as it turned out — thirty years can have that effect — but veteran Ray Mah, at head table, provided a significant insight. "Yes, I remember Jim, How is he? When he was C.N.A. president, he asked me to ...." Me too, Ray. When he was C.N.A. president, Jim had written and asked me to head a revitalized Coin Week Canada; which, for Jim's two years in office, to the best of my ability, I did. Jim, in a word, knew how to delegate, to seek out the right person (in his perception), and to draw upon, and support, that person's strengths. Jim gives much credit to his "coin" employees, and rightly so. But, he chose them, and developed them. In just that may lie the key to much of his lifelong success.

When Jim Charlton was honoured with the J. Douglas Ferguson Award, C.N.A.'s highest recognition, in 1972, the citation which accompanied the gold medal touched on Jim's two areas of "distinguished service to Canadian numismatics." I quote:

"You are one of the few Canadians who has earned, and deserve, the designation 'professional numismatist' in the finest sense of that term. As a professional coin dealer for over twenty years you established a reputation for honesty and integrity that greatly added to the prestige of Canadian numismatics at home and abroad. Your influence was always a steadying factor on the commercial side of our hobby."

And as to the catalogues that serve to perpetuate the "Charlton" name:

"Your catalogues of Canadian coins, tokens and paper money have become the accepted standard throughout the world ... The publication of your annual catalogues had contributed more during the past two decades to the increased interest in numismatics as a popular hobby in Canada than any other single factor."

That was 1972. With Bill Cross at the helm at The Charlton Press, the tradition has continued, and the depth and breadth of numismatic coverage expanded. This pleases Jim, I know. Rightly, he holds in high regard the continuing efforts that — into a new millennium — bear the "Charlton" name.

Jim's catalogues, in the days of his authorship, were the most widely used of Canadian coin references — no doubt they still are. Such success invites healthy competition, and a scanning of bibliographic entries will will reveal competitors in both languages. I always liked the Taylor and James Guide Books (typically, Reference 89) for their readiness to go a bit afield (as with modern tokens) and sample where they couldn't complete. There is a legitimate question just what varieties and such a "standard" catalogue should include. I see, "A friendly debate," endorsed by Jim in the margin of the *Coin World* page (3 December 1969, p. 53) on which Canadian Section editor Frank Rose featured positions of William English and of Jim. "Numismatists Debate Canada Catalog Content." My own stand I think Jim would agree with. No catalogue — and no dealer or fellow-collector — is going to tell me what I collect or omit from my collection, but I do welcome competent guidance, informatively presented. Jim, at one point, shared with me correspondence from knowledgeable collectors whose views, with me, carry much weight — I was privileged to know both of them well.

On Jim's 1973 catalogue:

"This book has turned out to be by far the best thing that has happened to Canadian numismatics.

"The book as a whole is very complete in the fields of Canadian coins, tokens and paper money.

"Fred Bowman."

And, on Jim's 25th Anniversary Edition, released in 1976: "Last evening was a very happy one, as I went over it, page by page. Every edition is more complete than the one before.

"You really deserve all the nice things that have been said of your many fine achievements in numismatics.

"J. Douglas Ferguson."

Much of the information upon which Jim bases his tale is accessible elsewhere, though perhaps not as readily as might be wished. Some rather illuminating documents, accordingly, I have shared as appendices. A price list of Canadian stamps, coins, tokens and paper money, put out by a youthful Sheldon S. Carroll in 1938, is illuminating as to the pre-War state of the hobby, and might be hard to find (Appendix E). Jim's "Canada Coin Exchange" offerings of 1949 (Appendix F) and 1951 (Appendix G) also are revealing, as are his prices realized from C.N.A.'s 1954 convention auction (Appendix H). A complete listing of Jim's auctions have been added as Appendix K.

Our "Jim's Conventions" listing (Appendix C) identifies 47 Canadian Numismatic Association conventions to date — and Jim is the only one of us who was in attendance at them all. Such information is available elsewhere, of course, but I included it on noting that Jim's comprehensive pen listing had been carefully updated each year. Such conventions, clearly, remain a main feature of Jim's calendar year, even — perhaps especially — in "retirement" decades. Jim also observes the degree to which two coin clubs with which he maintains close links, Toronto and North York, both in Ontario, over the years have been prime sources of C.N.A. leadership.

The Sixties, when Jim was highly active, are remembered as the decade of proof-like sets, rolls, mint bags — and rampant and ill-advised "coin" speculation. The decade of teletype circuits, too, and Appendix I serves to recall the extent of "circuit" membership. A 1963 Canada Coin Exchange radio commercial is recalled, and reproduced in full, in Appendix J. Those with a highly developed feeling for numbers — the fiscal kind — will find a 49-year update of some Charlton Catalogue prices, as Appendix L.

"This book is mostly illustrations," you can say with some truth if you subscribe to the venerable equivalence of one picture and one thousand words. Photographs selected for use here have been chosen both for their reproduction potential (their original composition and their state of preservation) and for their potential to illuminate the life-long and many-faceted story being shared. Early photos from the Charlton family album, accordingly, are succeeded by revealing glimpses of Thirties and Forties life in Northern Ontario. Ice cutting at Chalk River — an improbable juxtaposition — is one that Jim took himself. The great range of photos from Jim's years "in business" reflects help from two publications that have known Jim particularly well. Chet Krause at *Numismatic News* and Beth Deisher at *Coin World* went to the files and shared some of their best. A few of the more recent pictures I was pleased to take in Ottawa and Oakville when Jim and I got together in furtherance of this project. In all, you will glimpse scores of personalities whose interest and activities touched on Jim's life and work

Jim has functioned effectively within the organizational framework of the Canadian Numismatic Association. In his *Canadian Numismatic Journal* series, "Flashback — Reminiscences," Geoffrey G. Bell treats Jim's term as national president (Reference 12). Indeed, the organization's first fifty years have been well chronicled by association historian and archivist Stan Clute, so we avoid undue duplication here.

You want the unique story of Jim Charlton and his lifelong adventure, and that we're committed to provide you. You'll find it in the pages to follow — in pictures and, essentially, in Jim's well-considered words.

CANADA

AND

NEWFOUNDLAND

PAPER MONEY

BY J. E. CHARLTON

❖

Published By

CANADA COIN EXCHANGE

BOX 35, TERMINAL A
TORONTO, CANADA

Printed in Canada

Canada and Newfoundland Paper Money (1866-1935)

II

Recollections and Reflections
of
James E. Charlton

1.

The Formative Years

James Edward Charlton was born in Toronto, Ontario,
26 July 1911. His father, Thomas, was born in Toronto, 12
July 1873, and died in Toronto, 3 June 1959. His mother was
born in Dublin, Ireland, 20 August 1872, immigrated to
Canada (with the Williams family) in 1884, and died in
Toronto, 18 December 1952.

Autobiographical notes.

I grew up in a family of three girls, all older, an older
brother and a brother who was younger by two years. My
father was an architect, builder, and carpenter, and despite
the lean war years of 1914-1918 and the Great Depression
years, starting in 1930, he was able to provide for the large
household. Of course, like other families, we experienced little
in the way of luxuries during the war years, and practiced
economies in many ways. These included using
oleomargarine instead of butter, powdered milk ("Klim") in
place of fresh milk, and preserving eggs in isinglass. Our flock
of chickens was less productive during the winter months. A
roasted chicken dinner was usually on the weekend menu.
Various fruits were preserved by mother, and crab apple jelly
was popular as well. A large barrel of Northern Spy apples
would last throughout the winter months. Coal and coke
could represent major expenditure, so bins usually were filled
during the summer at discounted prices. Ashes would be
sifted to permit reuse of any unburned coal. Grocery stores
received much of their supplies in wooden boxes, and
householders found the wood useful as kindling or as a
supplementary fuel. One week in the 1920s, the road bed for
the streetcar tracks on Queen Street (at the bottom of
Sprucehill Road) was being repaired, and the old, heavily
tarred wooden blocks discarded. This was a real bonanza, as
they were high in B.T.U.'s. Our wheelbarrow was put to good
use in conveying the blocks to our cellar.

The Charlton family residence at 21 Sprucehill Road, in the Toronto east end district known as The Beaches, 1911 - 1963.

Jim (right) with Herb, his younger brother by two years. The boys were closely associated during their school days.

With Lil, youngest sister, at Thessalon, Ontario, about 1937.

A Charlton family picnic, Kew Gardens, Toronto. Jim's father and mother are on the left. Mary is in the middle surrounded by Jim's brothers and sisters and their children..

Two families: Mrs Tyndall, Mary's mother; Jim and Mary; Jim's mother and father with, behind them, Colonel J. Tyndall, Mary's father.

In 1911, our family moved to 21 Sprucehill Road in the Toronto east end — known as Balmy Beach. The property was to remain in the family for over 50 years. I was only six months old when we moved in, and it was my home for nearly 22 years. The large, two-storey, seven-room house was on a good size lot, with a three-car garage and a chicken coop. Sprucehill Road was a short, tree-lined street. The public school, with kindergarten and Grades I to VI, was at the top end.

Lake Ontario, with over a mile of beach and waterfront, was within easy walking distance. So, from 1907 to 1925, was the Scarboro Beach Amusement Park. Also reachable on foot were Balmy Beach, Kew Gardens Park, and (until 1929) the Glen Stewart nine-hole golf course.

Nearby, too, was Williamson Road School, where we completed Grades VII and VIII. Our high school was Malvern Collegiate, on Malvern Avenue, north of Kingston Road.

The area was known as Upper Beach. For a number of years the Malvern Junior Football Team was the best in Toronto. Some of the key players such as Yip Foster and Mansel Red Moore later joined the Balmy Beach Canoe Club team in the old Ontario Rugby Football Union, and helped it to win the Grey Cup. Balmy Beach won the cup in both 1927 and 1930.

In retrospect, I couldn't have chosen a better place to spend my childhood. In the words of a song of those years, "We didn't have much money, but we had lots of fun." Two other songs of the Twenties were "Yes, we have no bananas, we have no bananas today" and "Barney Google, with the goo, goo, googly eyes." I remember these two because I was in a children's choir that was on Saturday night programs at the Scarboro Beach Amusement Park. Our payment was a strip of 10 or 12 tickets — for such rides as the roller coaster, shoot-the-chutes, merry-go-round, aerial swings, and tunnel-of-love or entrance to the fun house.

Herb, my younger brother (by two years), shared a room with me, and a close association extended to most of our activities. One of my earliest memories relates to a metal coaster wagon. It probably was about 1918, and the wagon was named an Artillery Wagon, and painted grey. Our parents having said that it was to be shared between us, we decided that one of us owned the front half, and the other owned the rear.

We always had enough to eat, but were encouraged not to waste food. It may have been due to war-related shortages and the need to conserve sugar, but I remember that each of us was given an egg cup of sugar at the beginning of the week, and it was to be the week's supply.

We didn't receive a weekly allowance in those days, but Herb and I earned pocket money in various ways. Collecting refundable pop bottles left behind after weekend picnics, shovelling snow, delivering groceries and caddying at the Scarboro and Cedarbook golf courses, these were proven money raisers. My first effort as an entrepreneur consisted of repainting used golf balls and selling them to Eaton's.

Sundays in our growing up years were days of rest, and most stores and theatres were closed and parks were unavailable for sports. The afternoon Sunday school we were encouraged to attend, then Herb and I would walk east on Queen Street to Fallingbrook Road and Mann's Bush. The so-called Hundred Steps (actually I counted 142) could be descended from Queen Street and Fallingbrook Road to the waterfront and beach, or they could be ascended from the beach, which did call for a bit more effort. Our parents were non-smokers and abstainers, and the three sons followed their example, and probably the daughters as well. One slight deviation occurred at Christmas, when an old English tradition, the blazing of the plum pudding with a little rum, was followed. Of course, lights on the room were extinguished at the time, and it was a memorable sight. Adding to the interest was the possibility of finding a silver 5¢ piece, wrapped in wax paper, in your slice of pudding. A time consuming labour of love, for most housewives, was the making of such puddings in those days!

Those years in Toronto's East End were, I see in retrospect, good years. There was little in the way of traffic in those early times. Only the occasional car or truck, but many horse-drawn wagons, delivering milk and bread, groceries, fruit and vegetables in season. A regular visitor was a man with a long beard, and wagon, who would announce his presence by calling out, "Rags, bones and bottles!" These and other nondescript articles would change hands for nickels and dimes, with bargaining sometimes involved.

Eaton's and Simpsons, Toronto's two large department stores, made daily deliveries on most streets, and there was noticeable difference in the colour of the horses. Eaton's were a dapple grey and Simpsons' a plain brown. Department store wagons, and their loads, in the main were relatively light, and had a single horse, as did wagons of the bakeries. Some dairies, with heavier wagons and loads, used two-horse teams. Due to distance, depots and stables sometimes were strategically located.

Some East End streets involved steep hills, and it was customary for such streets to be used only for descent. Also, a metal shoe or plate was fastened under of the rear wheels, to keep it from revolving and to reduce the thrust of the wagon. Draft horses such as Clydesdales, Belgians, and Percherons were used for such heavier loads as coal and freight. Drivers would have occasion to pause for refreshment. During such brief stops, a canvas nosebag of oats would be placed on the horse, and a rope and round metal weight would keep it from wandering. A pail of cold water would be available from a customer, or from a streetside fountain or trough provided by the city. One of these remained for many years afterwards, on Kingston Road, near Main Street and Southwood Drive.

Fire stations in the East End were located on Main Street, above Kingston Road, and Queen Street, near Woodbine Avenue. A long-ago visit to Fire Station No. 17, the one on Queen Street, I vividly recall. The magnificent horses were in their stalls, the harness hanging from the ceiling, ready to be lowered quickly when required. The bright red wagons, loaded with ladders, hose and other equipment, were ready for action. Of course, I had to have my turn at sliding down the brass pole from the second floor!

My favourite story book, as a little boy, was *Black Beauty*. As I grew older, such stories of adventure as Horatio Alger, Tom Swift, Frank and Dick Merriwell, were my reading of choice.

The "Tunnel of Love" was one of the more popular Scarboro Beach attractions, at least with young adults. The "ride" of five minutes or so was the classic boat trip through a dark or dimly illuminated passageway. At intervals there would be brightly lighted scenic exhibits. A miniature steam railway was another ever-popular attraction.

Games of chance, or perhaps skill, included such as a mechanical rabbit race, bowling alley, fish pond and tossing balls into numbered compartments and rolling coloured balls into corresponding coloured holes. Also featured was a shooting gallery — with live ammunition.

The Penny Arcade, as the name implied, charged one cent for the likes of games, movies, and postcard-size sports cards. The "movies," in fact, consisted of a large number of cards, on a wheel, inside of a wooden cabinet the size of a large, old phonograph. After the depositing of the cent, the interior of the cabin would light up, and you would see the action through the viewing glass on the top of the cabinet. A hand control permitted the viewer to vary the speed of the action by speeding up or slowing down the wheel flipping the cards.

Very little in the way of out-of-school organized sports was available to us when I was growing up. Softball, hockey and football we could take part in by forming our own teams and playing against each other on Saturdays or at other convenient times. Equipment never was a problem, as little was required, and that would be available at minimum cost. For softball, only a bat and ball were needed — no gloves in those days. Hockey called for skates and boots, stick and puck. Used magazines often served as shin pads, and the goal line substituted for a net. Ice time would be available at the local pond, skating rink or hockey space. Football was called rugby, and a ball normally was all that was needed to get into play. Despite the total absence of the range of special equipment that would be deemed mandatory today, I don't recall any serious injury in our activities.

Golf my brother and I learned to play by caddying at the old Cedarbrook Golf and Country Club, then situated at Markham Road and Lawrence Avenue, Scarboro. For 18 holes, caddies were paid 50¢ — plus, sometimes, tips. Also, before members arrived in the morning, we were permitted to play the first two holes. I then moved on, to the more prestigious Scarboro Golf and Country Club (which backs on Markham Road), and was promoted to First Class Caddie, meaning that I'd receive 60¢ for 18 holes.

While, at Scarboro, caddies were not permitted early-morning play, they did have a "special day," once a season. On that day, we were allowed to use a member's set of clubs and play 18 holes in the morning, competing for prizes. Also, we would have use of the men's club house facilities, including the swimming pool. We then would enjoy a fine dinner.

Phil Farley, one of my fellow-caddies at Cedarbrook, went on to become one of Canada's best amateur golfers. Although I never came close to his stature as a golfer, I did have the interesting experience of competing with him in several tournaments. At the 1935 Burlington Golf and Country Club Invitational Tournament, Farley won the silver platter for low gross, and I won the silver platter for low net.

Miniature or Tom Thumb golf was a particularly popular pastime back in 1929, with many courses on vacant lots or inside buildings. Herb and I won the junior and senior championships of the Beaches, and I was second to Farley — by a stroke — at another tournament.

In addition to the golf, I took part in the Beaches two-mile road race, and also the Bloor Street Businessmen's two-mile competition.

The Humber River two-mile swim, between Bloor Street and Lake Ontario, I also participated in. In 1931, I believe it was, I was awarded a bronze medallion.

It was my real privilege to see the greatest of Canadian athletes, Lionel Conacher, close up and in action at Scarborough Beach Athletic Park in the early Twenties. Conacher was a star player for the Toronto Maitlands lacrosse team. Games frequently were played on Saturday afternoons. There was a club house for the players' privacy, and change rooms. Much of the time when the players were off the field was spent outside the club house, however, providing opportunity for fans to get close to the players. Also, when riding the roller coaster in the adjoining amusement park, it occasionally was possible to get a glimpse of Conacher and other players at practice. Conacher, I recall, went on to even greater renown as an outstanding player in three other popular team sports: football (Toronto Argos), baseball (Toronto Hillcrests) and hockey (Montreal Maroons). These are things that you recall and reflect upon, after all these years.

In 1928 I was employed in the office of Rous and Mann Printers, on Simcoe Street, just north of Queen Street, in downtown Toronto. One morning I was sent with a printer's proof to a photoengraving plant two blocks away. Instead of going to the front office directly, I decided to enter through the rear door, to view something of the operations. A short, plump man noticed my entrance, and beckoned me over to his workplace. He then asked me if I could put a coin on my forehead and drop it into a funnel. At the time, I noticed a number of his fellow employees were beginning to gather around, and I sensed an ulterior motive. I told the man that I thought that I could do that trick, but that I first had to deliver the printer's proof to the front office The proof was in a large manila envelope, and after making the delivery I would return with the empty envelope in my hand. By this time, we were encircled by about 15 employees. At that point, I asked for a demonstration.

"Sure," he responded. "You take a large funnel, and put the spout under the top of your trousers, like this. Then, you put your head back, and place a nickel on your forehead, and ...."

At this point, I poured a glass of cold water down the funnel, the spout of which was under the top of his trousers.

I then hurried out the back door ... never to return to that plant.

The glass of water I'd been able to keep hidden behind the manila envelope.

We live and Learn.

From December 1928 to August 1929, I was employed by the Miller Lithographic Company, at 100 King Street West, in downtown Toronto. At that time, the Toronto Star Building was being erected at 80 King Street West. During my noon hours, I would frequently visit the site, keenly observing the progress of the 21-storey building, to serve as the printing plant for the *Star* and *Star Weekly*, and in its early days, to house a radio broadcasting station. Miller Lithographic supplied Post Office Money Orders, which were imprinted for every post office in Canada; also, such as labels for food cans. The Standard Bank of Canada had been a customer. Following its merger with Canadian Bank of Commerce in 1928, we were using such leftover stationery as deposit slips for scratch pads.

I left Miller Lithographic soon afterwards, and several years later, around 1932, was to visit the Toronto Star Building during a field trip with a class of stationary

A Northern Ontario landmark, the International Nickel Smelter, as it appeared when Jim snapped this photo in May 1937.

Sudbury in the mid-thirties — note the characteristic vegetation — with a friend's splendid St. Bernard companion.

Sergeant Jim Charlton, Sault Ste. Marie Sudbury Regiment, M.G.C., Militia, 1938.

Jim Charlton, in 1939, a local officer of the Salvation Army Church.

Rails moves North and West. Canadian Pacific locomotive 2846 pulls Train No. 1, the Transcontinental, westbound from Montreal into Sudbury in January 1938.

engineers. It was an interesting experience to view the then completed and fully functional modern office building and newspaper plant.

My next return to the Toronto Star Building was in 1948, when I was employed, as Chief Engineer. It had been an interesting and unusual cycle: 20 years since my first visit in 1928.

A number of things have occurred during my lifetime that have appeared unimportant at the time but have turned our to be most significant. I will reveal some of these as they come to mind. In September, 1929 I was unemployed, and my elder brother, Harry, who was working for C.N.R. as a telegraph operator, mentioned a vacancy for an express clerk at the Riverdale Station in Toronto. I was hired and employed there until June, 1930. A decision was then made to have all express handled at the Union Station, so I was again unemployed. I took things easy for a few months with part time jobs, but getting into winter decided it was time to be gainfully employed. Incidentally, this was the only occasion in forty years that I was out of work. Again, it was my elder brother, Harry, who helped me to find a job. He suggested that I visit a new dairy in the west end of Toronto, Roselawn Dairy, and apply for a position as a salesman. At that time there were about fifty dairies delivering milk door to door in Toronto, many from horse-drawn wagons. E. T. Stephens, the owner of the new dairy, had a large farm at Richmond Hill, north of Toronto, and a herd of 300 Jersey cows, with a bull direct from Jersey that had cost $25,000, a lot of money in those days.

Dairies paid for milk on the basis of butterfat content, and as Jersey cows give less milk but higher butterfat, Stephens was paid a higher rate. However, the dairies required only a small amount of Jersey milk to bring the mostly Holstein milk up to the required standard. Holstein cows give large quantities of milk which has a low content of butterfat. Stephens was told that he no longer could be paid the high premium for all his milk, so he started his own dairy. I received a rather cold reception by the sales manager. He asked if I had sales experience, and I said no. He said, apparently to end the interview, that he didnt feel that I was capable of the position. My reply was that it was unfair to condemn a man without a trial. He said that that was a good point, and for me to report for work the next morning.

It was an interesting experience for a couple of weeks. The sales manager had a new Essex car, and we started out with several cases of Jersey milk. I believe the dairies were selling regular milk at 12¢ a quart. Roselawn Jersey milk was being offered at 11¢ a quart. This, for us, was a good sales advantage; and, in addition, we demonstrated how rich the cream was. These were the days before homogenized milk, and cream came naturally to the top. With a plastic tube and rubber washer forced down into the neck of the bottle, cream would be siphoned out and whipped with an egg beater. Sales of tickets, and new customers, developed rapidly, and to such an extent that there was not enough Jersey milk. A regular grade, called "Safe Milk," then was made available at the same low price, with the Jersey milk at a little higher price.

With the expanding business, additional inside employees were required, and I accepted an inside job that lasted from December 1930 to August 1933. During that time, I learned the dairy business inside and out and from top to bottom. With outside sales I already was well acquainted. Inside work included checking the 8 gallon cans of milk (this was before tank trucks): each can had to be checked, by smelling, before being dumped into the large pan on a weigh scale, and pumped upstairs to pasteurizing vats. Also, testing the milk for butterfat content, pasteurizing, bottling, cold storage, separating milk for cream, making buttermilk, operating machines for washing cans and bottles, and operating refrigeration machinery and a steam boiler.

The work was interesting, but the pay was somewhat low: only $17, and this for a week of seven days. After six months, however, employees were given a half day off each week. A year later, this was increased to a full day. The only exception was the stationary engineer, there being no one with the required engineer's certificate to take his place. I had been assisting him, and it was his suggestion that I take a course at the Central Technical School, write the examination, obtain the certificate and replace him on his day off. This would mean working a full day at the Dairy, having supper and then going to the School for two hours, two nights a week, for two winters. This I did, and was successful, obtaining a Fourth Class Certificate after the first year, and a Third Class after the second year.

A Toronto Police auction and a successful bid of $15 (this was, I believe in 1930), got me my first car, a so-called Small Six Studebaker, although it actually was a big four-door sedan. The car really was in running condition, and I had it for about a year. An early winter freeze, without adequate antifreeze, broke the engine block, unfortunately, and the car went to the wrecker, for $10.

While employed at the Roselawn Dairy, I was pleased to encounter a Big Six Studebaker. That car had previously served the dairy owner for holiday journeys to and from Florida. It later had had its back seat removed, and had been relegated to temporary delivery of cases of bottled milk which had been piled up in the back. Despite being the size of a truck, and having a truck's apparent strength, the car, or certainly its hindmost portions, had failed to measure up. After frequent repairs, the Big Six was retired from its onerous task.

When "Jack Kent Cooke" made headlines, it brought back boyhood memories. I'd known him as Jack Cooke during our school days. We both had lived in Balmy Beach, and both had attended Balmy Beach Public School, Williamson Road Public School and Malvern Collegiate. We participated in friendly games of softball, football and hockey.

Cooke was quite an enterprising young man, and got his real start in business in North Bay. He purchased a quantity of radios in the 1930s, but found it difficult to sell them because of lack of local reception. He then started his own station, sold the radios, and subsequently moved back to Toronto, where he took over CKEY.

He also, in due course, acquired *Liberty* magazine and the Toronto Maple Leaf baseball team.

Cooke was unsuccessful in his bid for a television license, and moved to the United States.

Although not an athlete himself, Cooke, throughout his life, retained great interest in organized sports.

He died recently, leaving an estate worth U.S. $800 million.

Many numismatic students, numismatic professionals and collectors were introduced to the hobby when someone gave them an old or unusual coin. That was my experience in 1926, and at 15 years of age, when Harry, my elder brother, who was a salesman for the Farmers Dairy in Toronto, gave me an 1863 Indian Head cent. It differed from Canadian large and small cents and United States Lincoln cents that I was familiar with, and its age fascinated me. Soon afterwards, I visited the stamp and coin store of George Lowe in downtown Toronto — on Adelaide Street, across from the old Adelaide Street Post Office. I told Mr. Lowe that I had a dollar to spend on a coin, and that I wanted the oldest that he had at that price. He soon produced an ancient Roman coin, 1,600 years old, and I was delighted. I still have it.

Although my funds were limited, coins could be obtained at bargain prices from second-hand stores in downtown Toronto — around Queen and York streets. One or two saucers of coins might be in the windows, pieces priced at 15¢ and 25¢ each. I was mostly interested in the old and unusual coins, and selected Canadian tokens, United States Civil War pieces, United States Hard Times tokens and such other obsolete United States coinage as half cents, large cents, two cents, three cents and half dimes. I knew of no reference book except for Mehl's Rare Coin Value Guide and of no active coin club. Accordingly, my collection or accumulation grew but slowly, but was of great interest to me, and was frequently shown to relatives and friends.

During the past 50 years I have handled a great deal of Canadian coinage and paper money, both rare and common issues. It is not easy to pick favourites in each category, but my choice in coins would be a large cent and in paper money the Canadian Bank of Commerce $10 note, dated 1892 and overprinted "Yukon."

While most of the large cents are still fairly common and inexpensive — they circulated well into World War II — the various issues and attractions and, for me, serve to bring back fond memories.

The large cent is the first coin I remember from my early school years. It was, after all, all that was required to have a choice from a great variety of "cent" candy. The candy was produced by the Robertson Brothers factory, on the south side of Queen Street, between Church and Jarvis streets, in downtown Toronto. During the early post-war inflation, "cent" candy disappeared, and also the company. The huge, five-storey building currently is used for offices, warehousing and other business activities.

The large cent also proved useful at the Penny Arcade in the Scarborough Beach Amusement Park, operating many an entertainment or vending machine.

Occasionally a large cent would be placed on a streetcar track and flattened ... for a souvenir.

We were encouraged, of course, to practice thrift by putting our coins, usually large cents, in a piggy bank, or depositing them weekly at school, to be credited to our account at the downtown Penny Bank. The Institution no longer is in operation.

In paper money, my treasured possession for many years was my Canadian Bank of Commerce $10, 1892 issue, with the bold "Yukon" overprint. It not only is old and interesting, but is historic in commemorating the Trail of '98. It was there. It actually was one of the notes in the first shipment on that perilous journey to the Yukon. This was verified by the bank, through checking of the signatures and serial number. I realized after an article that I wrote for a newspaper that it was quite a rare note. Neither the Canadian Bank of Commerce nor the Bank of Canada Numismatic Collection had a note of the particular type, and interest was expressed in mine. I loaned the Commerce the note to photograph, and after some years agreed to transfer my note to the Bank of Canada museum collection. It will now have a lot more visibility than I was able to provide.

2.

Northern Ontario Commitments
(1933-1948)

My 15 years — including the War years — of strategic and responsible work in Northern Ontario began in the simplest possible way.

In July 1933, my youngest sister, Lillian, who was a school teacher in Northern Ontario, was married, and after a honeymoon visited the family home in Toronto prior to returning North. It just happened that I was about to start my week's holiday. Lillian and her husband, Syd Jones, invited me to journey with them and to spend the week with them at their cottage near Thessalon, east of Sault Ste. Marie. I accepted the invitation, and enjoyed the drive and the visit. It was the first time that I had been past Huntsville.

I was impressed with the scenery. Also, with the massive International Nickel smelter and copper refinery plants at Copper Cliff, a few miles west of Sudbury. I got to thinking that there could be stationery engineers required for such industries, and decided to find out if there might be an opening for me. My Third Class certificate qualified me for more responsibility that the dairy position, which called for only the Fourth Class. Upon my return to Toronto, I wrote to the Inco smelter and copper refinery; also to the Inco nickel refinery at Port Colborne and Falconbridge Nickel Company. Within two weeks, I had replies from three of the companies. None had a vacancy. I was a little disappointed, but at least appreciated the replies. Nothing had been received from the copper refinery. However, soon afterwards I had a telephone call from a Mr. Kitchener, chief engineer at the Inco Ontario (Copper) Refinery. He had received my query, and was in Toronto on vacation, and wished to meet with me. In the course of an hour he was at my residence, and in another hour I had a job. The 45¢ an hour offer was an improvement over the dairy, particularly as there had been the frequent seven-day weeks. The dairy manager had asked if I would consider staying if given the stationery engineer job. Of course, I refused.

From August 28, 1933 to January 14, 1940, I was employed at the copper refinery: operating the coal pulverizing plant (pulverized coal was used in copper furnaces

Visitors to Capreol, Ontario in 1939, King George VI and Elizabeth, the present Queen Mother.

The Royal couple and the mayor of Capreol, in a candid photo by a bystander.

Joe Laflamme's team of wolves which he had trained to pull a sled. Sudbury, in 1939.

Thomas Charlton — Jim's father — the builder, and church members at the site of the Manse being put up for the new paster of the United Church of Canada. Levack, Ontario, 20 October 1940.

Out of the wilderness, "Silverbirch Avenue" Nobel, Ontario, has its beginnings in April 1942, with some of 200 new houses nearing completion.

which held 325 tons of copper), tending large steam boilers, maintenance of boilers and air compressors, and assisting in the power house. A first class engineer broke a rule by going behind the electrical panel, and suffered severe burns and shock from current at high voltage. He survived, but as an additional warning to others, the rubber mat, with imprints of his feet in melted rubber, was placed at an entrance to the control room.

It was quite an experience for me to be in Sudbury. I lived temporarily in a room over a restaurant, until I found room and board with a nice family for most of the seven years. Working an eight-hour shift left time for golf, swimming in Lake Ramsay, ice skating and membership in the militia.

Two experiences from my first winter I particularly remember. With the first cold weather, Lake Ramsay was like a giant skating rink, and I couldnt resist the urge to skate the perimeter. Despite my good physical condition, my leg joints were stiff for a few days afterwards. Trolley cars in Sudbury provided transportation to and from the refinery and smelter, apart from a short walking distance between the stations and the plants. One beautiful clear morning in the early winter, in my youthful exuberance I decided to jog instead of walking. This resulted in a frozen nose. The temperature had been lower than realized. The coldest weather I experienced in Sudbury was 64 below zero Fahrenheit.

Sudbury, like other mining communities, had a population made up mostly of single men, and quite a number participated in sports. In fact, some obtained employment due to their athletic ability, while others joined various service organizations, which included the local militia.

One Saturday night I was in the Old Post Office building in downtown Sudbury. Hearing music, I look out of the window, and saw a group of young people from the Salvation Army Church, with their brass band instruments, having an open air meeting. I was favourably impressed with the street meeting, and accepted the invitation to attend the indoor service at their nearby church. It was a friendly happy fellowship, and provided an opportunity for me to make a small contribution by participating in various activities in the days that followed.

This was interrupted when I was transferred, in January 1940 to Inco's Levack Mine, some distance from Sudbury.

The move came after my success in obtaining a second class Stationary Engineer's certificate, and with a chief boiler room engineer being required at Levack. This was a better position, and all day shifts. Accommodation was to be in a modern hotel, with meals and a private room.

There was a community church in Levack, with a circuit pastor who was responsible for three Sunday services, one in each community. Due to a change in pastors, there would be an interval of two months that summer without a pastor at Levack. I was asked to fill in, and did so. After the new preacher, Reverend G. H. Corscadden, arrived, a Church Executive Committee was formed, and I was elected chairman. It was decided to build a manse in Levack. The committee chose my father to provide the plans and construct the building.

I left Levack to work in Nobel on 20 October 1940.

My seven years in the Sudbury area I was without a car, there being no particular need for one. Traveling back and forth to Copper Cliff was by trolley car, or else pooled transportation. There was bus service between Sudbury and Levack.

At Nobel, I made frequent trips to Parry Sound, a distance of seven miles, and occasionally I went to Toronto, 165 miles. Accordingly, a car was purchased on one of my excursions from Nobel to the city, a used car, a 1928 Chevrolet coach that cost me $80. For about two years, it let me down only once — a frozen gas line. However, the weekend of 19 December 1942, I'm not likely to forget. Saturday evening was distinctly cold, and I was able to leave the car in a heated garage, until my 6:15 departure. The temperature in Nobel was minus 20 degrees Fahrenheit, and Highway 69 was icy. A manifold heater from the engine block was to be the sole source of warmth. On short trips and at moderate temperatures it had proved to suffice, but I soon sensed that this was to be a perilous night. The temperature seemed to be falling, and I wondered how long I'd survive if the car were to leave the icy road.

Other traffic on the road was virtually nil. At the ever lower temperatures, the car heater was proving to be all but useless, and my feet were decidedly cold,

With 165 miles to go, I knew I'd require several stops to get thawed out and refreshed. My first stop, and most welcome one, was at Gravenhurst and Highway 11. Next was Beaverton. Then Whitby. And, finally, Toronto, at 2:45, Sunday morning. A hot chocolate at each stop had added to the time, and 8 ½ hours was about twice the normal duration for the Toronto trip.

It was time to get a newer and better car, needless to say, I was convinced. My choice was a nice looking 1936 Ford Coach. I had been told that Ford cars, in those days, could be heavy on oil. This car, the salesman assured me, would be an exception. I believed him. I paid about $400, and was delighted with the performance as I traveled from Toronto back to Nobel. As I stopped for gas at Gravenhurst, about 100 miles from Toronto, I thought to have the oil level checked. Oil level? It had disappeared, I was shocked to find out. After a valve and ring job, the car was in good shape, and my only problem would be a leaking radiator, after several years.

During the War, and for several years afterwards, it was very difficult to purchase a new car, without paying a substantial premium above the legitimate retail price. My first new car, a Chevrolet sedan Biscayne, I bought in 1951. Since then, I have owned various makes and models, usually keeping a car for three years.

In 1940 I was Chief Boiler Room Engineer at the Levack Mine of International Nickel Company, and was living in the nearby townsite of Levack.

One day, all residents received notice to boil the tap water before drinking it or using it for cooking. Due to a ruptured water line, a temporary connection would be made for a supply of untreated water for most of the week.

Fortunately, however, a few of us knew of an alternative source of unsurpassed drinking water. Alongside a little used road by the townsite there was a spring of clear, cold water, coming out of a gravel bank.

After a hot day in the boiler room and the walk back to the townsite, nothing ever was more desirable and refreshing than a drink of the cold spring water.

I was in Northern Ontario from 1933 to 1948, during which years there were important numismatic occurrences. For the most part, however, there was little, of any, activity in organized Canadian numismatics. I am, however, recalling some of the numismatic, or monetary, milestones with which this interval can be identified.

1933. Canadian Antiquarian and Numismatic Journal. Final issue.

1934. Bank of Canada created as the Nation's central bank and bank of issue.

1935. The end of silver dollar coinage in the United States. The start of the corresponding Canadian series.

Release of the first issue of Bank of Canada notes.

1936. Toronto Coin Club organized. Understood to be Canada's oldest continually operating numismatic organization.

"Dot" coinage, in 1¢, 10¢, 25¢ denominations. Not recognized until years later.

1937. The Coronation. New "King George VI" coinage and notes.

Wayte Raymond's Coins and Tokens of Canada, first edition, prices by types, not dates.

1938-1939. Bert Koper, Winnipeg barber and enthusiastic collector, started Canadian Numismatic Coin Topics. Familiar names appeared in its pages: Maurice Gould, Professor Prince (of Truro), J. D. Ferguson, Sheldon Carroll. Koper also published booklets on the varieties of Canadian cents of 1858 and 1859 and of the tombac 5¢ pieces of 1942 and 1943. His efforts were started at an inopportune time, and became casualties of World War II.

1940-1944. No silver dollars struck during these war years. Tombac 5¢ struck in 1942 and 1943. Plated steel 5¢ struck in 1944 and 1945.

1941. Prices realized at Max Mehl's auction of Dunham collection: Br 564, Owen Ropery, VF, $38; Br 925 North West, VF, $40; Br 956, Peter McAusland, EF, $15.25; Br 525, Side View Penny, AU, $52.50; Br 1000, Ships, Colonies & Commerce, large ship, VF, $52; Br 973, Wellington half penny, VF, $22.

1944. New York dealer Hans Schulman, Catalogue 25, lists Courteau collection, which included rare tokens: 5 sols of 1670, $15; 15 sols of 1670, $500; Side View Penny, $135; bridge tokens, $16 to $75 each; Hunterstown half penny, $52.50; 50¢ pieces different dates, F, 60¢, and UNC, $1.20.

1945. Glendining sale, London, England, of the Dr. Brushfield collecion: 5 sols of 1670, VF $37; proof sets of 1911 and 1921, of 5¢, 10¢, 25 ¢, and 50¢, plus silver dollars of 1935 and 1936, $25. One of the great bargains. Norman B. Mason's mail bid was unsuccessful.

1947. Wayte Raymond's Coins and Tokens of Canada, second edition, listes coinage by dates, mint marks, mintages and gives values. A big improvement over the 1937 edition, and a major contribution to Canadian popular numismatics.

Fred Bowman's survey of Decimal Coinage of Canada and Newfoundland, in the March *Numismatist*, and subsequently as an American Numismatic Association special publication. Another major contribution.

The start of an institution, Chet Krause's Introductory Issue of *Numismatic News* dates back to 1952.
Jim long advertised and promoted "Canadian" collecting in such U.S. periodicals.

3.

Toronto, *The Star*, and the Coin Business

STEAM ENGINEER

For industrial boiler plant. Must have first class papers
and technical training.... Please give full details of education,
experience and salary required to Box 2515, *Star.*
27 December 1947.

Answering a small classified ad in the *Toronto Star* while in Toronto for Christmas was to turn my life in a new direction.

I commenced employment at the *Star* in April 1948. Shortly after my arrival, three of us — Burnett Thall, a consulting metalurgist; Raymond Matheson, the plant superintendnt; and I — made arrangements to attend a power show in New York City. Our schedule called for Air Canada departure — T.C.A. in those days — in the early evening of what turned out to be a rainy and foggy day. With the unpromising weather, actual departure was uncertain until shortly before flight time. With some apparent improvement, our taking off was confirmed, and we boarded the North Star. It was my first flight and, visibility still being quite limited, I had some reservations about safety. However, the pilot revved up the engines, and soon we were airborne. I had a window seat, and after a few minutes looked out, surprised to see a clear sky and the stars. I commented to Burnett that it was remarkable how the weather had changed so quickly. He pointed out that we were above the clouds.

J. E. Atkinson, founder of the *Toronto Star*, died in 1948, and his son, J. S. Atkinson, succeeded him. It was apparent that the ability of Burnett Thall was recognized in his early association with the *Star*, and in 1948 he was given an office adjoining that of the publisher. I found it gratifying to follow his continuing successful career. At the time of my departure, I was called into his office for a farewell and a generous retainer fee. This was unexpected, but appreciated, as had been the earlier payment of moving expenses from Deep River, in 1948, without any agreement. I found the *Star* to be an excellent employer in every way, and only left because the growing coin business required my full time.

Wedding photo, Jim and Mary, 2 March 1945 — "an easy date to remember, 2/3/45."

With son Jim, Jr., who went on to a career in printing. Deep River, in 1946.

The Charlton residence in Deep River — the upper left apartment.

Wartime housing, Nobel, Ontario, 1945.

Something that you do see in mining areas, a house being moved, from Nobel to Deep River, in 1945.

As chief engineer of the Toronto Star building, I had responsibility for such as heating, air conditioning, ventilation, compressed air and water systems. An interesting aspect of the job was to see the different components of the newspaper contributing to publication on a daily basis.

Of J. E. Atkinson, the paper's founder, it was said that he made rules, and expected them to be kept. Sometimes, however, they were violated at his own discretion. One, when an executive hinted that something that Atkinson was doing was breaking his own rules, Atkinson responded: "It's against the rule, yes, but some of my rules are like carpenters rule's: they have hinges in them. But any member of staff pleading "hinges" had to have a good reason to back him up.

J. E. Atkinson forbid the term "deaf and dumb" to be used in the paper. He had a hearing impairment himself.

Some people you remember ... and remember:

While I was chief engineer at the *Toronto Star*, at 80 King Street West, the *Star* also had a 99-year lease on the property at 1 Yonge Street, and my responsibilities included supervision of the steam boilers at that location. On the afternoon of Marilyn Bell's historic swim of Lake Ontario, I was on my to the boiler room at 1 Yonge Street for a routine visit.

I had picked up an afternoon edition of the *Star*, and was walking south on the west side of Bay Street. As I emerged from the underpass south of Front Street, I noticed the headline on the *Star* front page — and a progress report on the courageous effort being made by the 16-year-old swimmer. I was profoundly moved, and uttered a silent prayer for her. I see by the *Star* (George Gamester's Column, 16 August 1994, p. A4) that Marilyn, now a grandmother, lives — and swims — in a New Jersey retirement community.

The direction of our lives can be influenced by matters quite beyond our immediate control, we realize. When I returned to Toronto early in 1948, I found that the city had changed greatly during my North Country sojourn. There were new buildings, and great development in the suburbs. However, despite the many signs of prosperity, I encountered indications that not all was well. For example, the Concourse Building, a high-rise office building of some 20 storeys which had been nearing completion on Richmond Street West, had been a victim of the 1930s Depression, and was not completed and occupied until some years later. Another such victim was the luxury Park Plaza Hotel, at Bloor and Avenue Road, which was not completed and opened until many years afterwards.

The heating system at the Toronto Star Building was not the most modern, and I was asked to check out one of the very latest designs, in Detroit. It was in a large office building — the Barlum Tower, as I recall. On my return, I was able to present a favourable report. During my stay in Detroit, however, I observed the skeleton of a high-rise office building, another reminder of the 1929 Disaster in 1949.

One of my shift engineers had mentioned losing property due to nonpayment of taxes during the Depression. My father had lost property in Lake Worth, Florida, in the same way,

A coal salesman, one day, shared with me a chart which graphically portrayed business cycles of the past couple of centuries. I found it intriguing how history had left a record of repeating itself — with prosperity after a war, followed by a recession or depression. That had been the case after the 1914-1918 War, and many anticipated a somewhat similar experience after 1939-1945. Fortunately, such did not occur, and a record interval of prosperity has been our lot.

During my many years with the *Star*, I had opportunity, over lunch times, to make numerous worthwhile contacts. One of these was C. S. Howard, then serving as managing editor of the *Canadian Banker*. Howard had his offices in the Royal Bank Building, just a block and a half from the *Star*. Howard's article on Canadian banks and bank notes, which had appeared in the *Canadian Banker*, was republished as a booklet of up to 46 pages. He had deemed it prudent to have much of the press run of the booklet stockpiled, and this, in retrospect, can be seen to have been a good decision. On one of my visits, I chanced to learn of the unbound pages, and suggested that additional illustrations be added to future releases of the publication. Ninety-six added note illustrations, as provided by J. Douglas Ferguson and myself, were incorporated into subsequent distributions.

During another of my visits, Howard told me that he had been present, as a witness, at the destruction by burning of bundles of Ontario Bank notes that had been redeemed by the Royal Trust Company. What a tragedy that was for Canadian paper money collectors!

On another such occasion, Howard had given me an uncut, printed sheet of Farmers Joint Stock Banking Company notes. These were on heavy, glossy paper, with denominations of $4, $4, $10 and $50. Apparently, a man had chanced upon the printing plate at a garbage dump.

About the same time, a veteran Toronto coin dealer gave me an uncut, printed sheet of Niagara District Bank bills. This "4/on" sheet comprised $4, $5, $5 and $10 notes. The printing plate had been found in an old cellar, and had been loaned to the dealer to run off a few copies.

As had many other coin dealers, I started as a collector, my collection of interesting but inexpensive coins growing slowly from 1927 to 1949. In the latter year, I learned that quantities of Canadian large cents, 5 cents silver, Newfoundland coins and large-size and other non-current bank notes, were being withdrawn by the banks and shipped to Ottawa for melting at the Mint or for burning. I had a good relationship with the tellers at the main bank branches and at the Bank of Canada in downtown Toronto, and a weekly noon hour visit usually would be rewarded with a variety of coins and notes. Included on occasion were some of Canada's key date coins.

In addition to such bank acquisitions, I was able to purchase the coin inventory of the York Stamp and Coin Company, then located on the second floor of the old Prince George Hotel Building, south-east corner of King and York streets. The owner had decided to change his *modus operandi* to a mail order stamp business operated from his residence.

My first mimeographed Price List was released late in 1949, and my first Mail Bid Auction list in May 1950. Mail bid auctions continued through the eighth, for 21 November 1953, with price lists at regular intervals.

My first public sale was C.N.A.'s 1954 convention auction, its first, at Toronto's King Edward Hotel. This was followed by additional C.N.A. auctions, through 1969 at the Royal York Hotel, the one exception being the 1963 in Vancouver, conducted by Robert Levy. The joint A.N.A.-C.N.A. convention of 1962, held in Detroit, featured an A.N.A. auction by Jim Kelly. I had the associated C.N.A. auction. A single auction catalogue covered the two sales.

From April 1948 through July 1956, during my *Toronto Star* employment, my coin business operated from my home, on a part-time basis, evenings and Saturdays. My wife, Mary, was a big help as the business secretary. As the *Star's* chief engineer, my assistant was Robert Clark, and an occasional switch in shifts would permit me an extended weekend to attend a convention.

The opening of a retail store, office and warehouse was necessitated by the rate of business growth, so the operation was relocated at 53 Front Street East on 2 August 1956. The move did much for the efficiency of the operation, and the addition of employees for the store, office and warehouse took care of the increased business.

The Front Street premises were generally satisfactory — apart from security. Returning from an A.N.A. convention one Monday morning, I found that the lock on the front wooden door had been removed with a saw, and that an office safe had been looted. Fortunately, a heavy-duty Taylor safe with gold coins and paper money had proven to be impenetrable, so the actual loss was limited to $3,000-$4,000, which was covered by insurance. Of course, some items can be difficult to replace. Following the burglary, I had an alarm system installed, and there was no repetition of the burglary.

However, that was not all. One Saturday afternoon I had what I think of as the most terrifying experience of my life. Mary and I, with two male employees, were on the Front Street office filling mail-orders when two masked men, with a loaded 38 revolver, entered the premises. Mary was shoved into a cupboard; one employee and I were forced to lie on the floor, and were tied up. The older employee, a retired policeman, told the masked men that he had a bad heart, so they let him stand. While one robber held the gun on us, the other was loading our inventory into a gunny-sack. To have a loaded gun pointed at my head was, for me, terrifying. When the gunman momentarily took his eyes off us, the retired policeman grabbed the gun, aimed and pulled the trigger twice. The gun failed to fire, and the robbers retrieved the weapon and pistol-whipped the retiree. While this was going on, a customer and his friend looked in the door, grasped what was happening, went back downstairs and had a storekeeper call the police. Two officers arrived quite promptly. The leading policeman ran into the back room. The unarmed rookie policeman came into the office and the armed gunman tossed his weapon behind the counter. Both robbers quite humbly surrendered.

I later asked my customer the purpose of his visit that day, and he said that it had been to purchase a 1948 silver dollar. I gave him one, with my compliments. Following that terrible experience, we relocated the business to 80 Richmond Street East, also in downtown Toronto, 31 October 1958.

The small three-storey building was purchased, and required extensive renovations to the first floor, which became the headquarters for Canada Coin Exchange. At the same time, it was possible to redesign the floor layout for the retail store, office and warehouse. The tenants of the two upper floors continued their leases.

Interest in numismatics was growing rapidly in the early Sixties, and our business in coins and collectors' accessories was more than keeping pace.

Although my employment at the *Toronto Star* and my efforts in the coin business both were enjoyable and interesting, together they made for a heavy work load, and I did look forward to Sundays. These, by choice, were days of rest from labour, but not for idleness. As a member of the Salvation Army, I attended and participated in the services.

Apart from the long weekday hours, I had to consider the lack of time with my family and the question of loyalty to my regular employer. A prestigious position and a company pension I would be giving up. In my opinion, however, with my then divided interest, such would be the honourable and moral thing to do, so I left the *Star* after 13 years with the best of employers.

Living in Toronto, I soon learned much from other collectors and part-time dealers. There was no full-time dealer for some years. I think I was the first one in Toronto. At the time it was customary for branch banks to send their obsolete coins, such as silver 5¢ pieces, and old bank notes, to main offices in Toronto. Shipments would then be made to Ottawa, where coins would be melted and government notes would be burned. I was able to obtain such material from friendly tellers. Soon, the problem was to dispose of it! I "wholesaled" thousands of large cents at 11¢ each for Queen Victoria and 6¢ each for Edward VII.

At one point a particularly colourful and distinctive hoard of Canadian notes came on the market. These were attractive $1, $2, $4 and $5 Bank of Brantford bills, the red tint version "payable" — if payable they truly had been — at Sault Ste. Marie. Such were unsigned, unissued "remainders," and several U.S. dealers were offering them. The engraving was pleasing, and such items have a history and frequently are popular with collectors. I acquired and sold a supply — which, as sets or individual notes, may persist in collections to this day.

Seymour Kazman, a Toronto stamp dealer, had a small store in the Yonge Street Arcade, at 137 Yonge Street, a good downtown location. At one point he invited me to share with him, with me selling coins and numismatic accessories. Each of us would have half the window, floor, wall and storage areas, and pay half of the rent. It appeared to be a good arrangement for both of us, and a deal was quickly consummated.

The store was narrow, perhaps 8 feet in width, which permitted two showcases and counters, lengthwise. Kazman generously permitted me to have my half of floor space at the front of the store, which allowed for the first showcase, counter and wall space.

Accordingly, our Arcade Coin Store, with Frank Rose as manager, opened in February 1963. Business exceeded expectations, and it was soon decided to move to a larger store, with more width, on the opposite side of the Arcade, with the same fifty-fifty deal.

The wider store was much better for both of us. It had a centre door entrance, between two separate display windows. Inside the store, the stamp business was on one side, the coin business on the other, with ample room in the centre for customers and for island displays. There also was space at the back of the store for additional showcases, wall displays and a storage room.

The year 1963 was a rather eventful one for me. In February I started the Arcade Coin Store business. In May the entire stock of International Coin Co., consisting of coins and coin and stamp accessories, was purchased. On June 26, Canada Coin Exchange opened, Toronto's newest coin store, at 49 Queen Street East, a good downtown address.

Atomic age meets ice age: cutting ice on the Ottawa River at the Deep River site, 1946.
Decades earlier, sawing would have been by hand.

Atomic power from horsepower? A horse-drawn sled hauls ice at Deep River, Ontario, in 1946.

In control. Jim at the Master Control panel in the Nobel, Ontario Power House. The year was 1942.

Jim, on return to Toronto, taking on senior engineering responsibilities at the Toronto Star.

International Coin Co., a division of Theatre Poster Service, had been a serious competitor in the philatelic and numismatic accessories business. With its purchase, we became the largest wholesale distributors of collector supplies in Eastern Canada.

Business once again was beyond expectations, and can be attributed to such factors as location, with exposure to heavy pedestrian traffic, and sales personnel. Frank Rose was an excellent manager, and was ably assisted by Richard Hazzard, a specialist in ancient coins, and Mary, my wife. This was the four and a half years between 1963 and 1968. In the latter year, Rose bought my interest in Arcade Coins. He continued the business successfully for further years, then decided on a change of *modus operandi*. He found a replacement for himself for the Arcade store, and re-established a business, Frank Rose Enterprises, in a downtown Toronto office. In addition to a retail coin business, Rose reactivated Torex, and from 1970 to 1978 held yearly Torex and other sales.

The most noteworthy of the Rose sales was that of the McKay-Clements numismatic collection, in 1976. This was a major, comprehensive offering of quality and rare Canadian numismatic material — such as the 1911 pattern silver dollar, which sold for $110,000. Other "coin" rarities included Canada's 1921 fifty cents, which brought $21,000, and 1921 silver five cents, which brought $5,200. In Canadian tokens, the 15 sols of 1670, Br 501, EF, at $10,000, was the best price, followed by the British Columbia pattern $20, Br 934, in silver gilt, $7,500; British Columbia pattern $10, Br 935, in silver gilt, $8,000; the bouquet sous, Br 67, VF $3,400.; Repentigny silver set of 12, proof, $3,750. One medallic classic, Br 90, 1867, silver, 3 inches, in case, sold for $2,400. In bank notes, top prices were paid for two chartered bank rarities, a United Empire Bank $10, 1906, fine (but a quarter inch tear), $3,200; and a Crown Bank $5, 1904, VF, $3,000.

Frank Rose, like myself, retired early. In the late 1970s he relocated to Boca Raton, Florida, about a mile from my winter residence in that city, It was a great shock and loss when Frank died suddenly, at the age of 57, in 1983. His contribution to the hobby had been substantial, and his reputation the highest.

Consolidation of the operations of the store and office at Queen Street and the warehouse on Richmond Street was decided upon, and was carried out in 1965 on purchase of a larger, four-storey building at 92 Jarvis Street, also in downtown Toronto. After necessary renovations and alterations were completed, the 4,000 square foot main floor served all purposes.

Although 1965 and 1966 were not good years for some coin dealers — a number went out of business — others, including ourselves, experienced a degree of success. Conditions were helped in 1967 by the release of Centennial coinage: it was difficult to meet the demand for plastic holders for the six-coin sets. In fact, our salesman had to wait with the van to pick up our order of mint set holders as they came off the production line.

I was enjoying the growing, three-fold business, but realized that it was consuming too much of my time, leaving little for my wife, Mary, and son, Jimmy. A Maritimer, a Mr. Forbes, bought the supply business. Along with its building, in July 1967. The Canada Coin business I relocated to an office in the Lumsden Building, corner of Yonge and Adelaide streets, still in downtown Toronto. As part of the Forbes deal, I was to continue as editor and publisher of the *Standard Catalogue of Canadian Coins, Tokens and Paper Money*.

Frank Rose acquired the Arcade Coin Store business in 1968. I wanted him to have it, and he wanted it, so no one else was considered in regard to the sale. In the meantime, I was carrying on with the Canada Coin Exchange business, including C.N.A. auction sales of 1964 to 1969 ... a follow-up to sales of 1954 through 1962.

I sold Canada Coin Exchange in 1969, but continued with editing and publishing of the *Standard Catalogue*.

The coin and stamp supply business was carried on for a few more years by Forbes; then, due to failing health, he sold out to William K. Cross. Part of the deal I had struck with Forbes included the name "Charlton" with the business. Cross wanted the name also, in his deal with Forbes. My permission was required, and I gave it, as a favour to both men. This agreement extended to the *Standard Catalogue of Canadian Coins*, which I edited until the 1980, 30th edition. After that edition, Bill Cross is responsible for all numismatic catalogues with the "Charlton" name.

During the 20 year operation of Canada Coin Exchange, 1949 to 1969, I was privileged to make many friends and to play an active role in many numismatic areas, both in Canada and beyond. The friendships I cherish, and a range of activities persist to enrich these "retirement" years.

The auction sales, public and mail bid, were a central, and particularly memorable, concern. Included were 15 C.N.A. convention auctions, Torex in 1962, Province of Quebec in 1962 and 1963, Empire State in 1964, plus a number of club shows.

A particular pleasure was attending and having a bourse table at major coin shows and conventions form coast to coast, in Canada and in the United States.

Appearances on television and radio programs — always a challenge — were, I believe, worthwhile.

Speaking engagements at conventions, coin shows, universities, school and history groups, provided a useful exchange of insights.

During those 20 years, I had the assistance of more than a dozen loyal, trustworthy staff members. Whatever success we achieved was, I know, due in large measure to them.

Now, after 20 and more years of retirement, I continue to find it a great pleasure to keep in touch with the numismatic scene.

4.

Catalogues ... and Numismatic Periodicals

Canada's Coin Bible, in the numismatic industry is, and
always has been, the Charlton Catalogue.
Don Thomas (Reference 92).

The *Catalogue of Canadian Coins, Tokens & Fractional Currency*, the 1952 1st edition, the first "Charlton Catalogue," was a modest effort of some 34 pages, with green paper covers. The effort was well received, however — it filled a need — and (apart from 1954) was updated in yearly revisions through 1959.

A major change in the catalogue dates from 1960 (8th) edition. Addition of government paper money issues of Canada and Newfoundland, resulted in renaming as the *Standard Catalogue of Canadian Coins, Tokens & Paper Money*. The catalogue had a modified format, new individual illustrations, additional information and an increase in pages to 126 ... as a very distinctive, blue cloth-bound coin book. Yeoman and Bressett were responsible for printing, sales and distribution by Whitman's Coin Products Division, for yearly editions to 1970 — which resulted both in increased catalogue sales and heightened interest in Canadian numismatics.

As the major Canadian distributor of Whitman coin products, I enjoyed an excellent relationship with them, as a consultant for their other specialized Canadian items — coin folders, albums and the like.

With the 1971 (19th) edition, I resumed publication. The book was enlarged to 200 pages, to incorporate note issues of Canadian and Newfoundland banks. After several further annual revisions, I turned publication, as such, over to William K. Cross, though I continued as editor through the 1980 (30th) edition. From the 1971 to 1978 revision, the catalogue had increased in size from 200 to 341 pages.

In his *Toronto Star* "Coins" feature in 1977, columnist Robert Aaron could allude to 1.25 million Charlton catalogue sales in the first 25 years of publication, and speak of the catalogues as, numismatically, the bible of Canadian collectors.

Another significant change to Charlton catalogue structuring came with the 1979 edition. *The Charlton Standard Catalogue of Canadian Coins* deleted the token and paper money content, which would be otherwise provided for, and this permitted an increase in background information on the coins. There were semi-annual releases of the Catalogue from 1979 to 1984, ten yearly editions, which continue. My editorship ended with the 1980 (30th) edition, though Bill Cross and I keep in touch, and I contribute input that seems pertinent.

The token and paper money "spin-offs": permitted careful treatment of these important areas, We now have the *Charlton Standard Catalogue of Canadian Colonial Tokens*, 4th edition, 236 pages; the *Charlton Standard Catalogue of Canadian Communion Tokens*, 2nd edition, 284 pages; the *Charlton Standard Catalogue of Canadian Government Paper Money*, 13th edition, 306 pages; and the *Charlton Standard Catalogue of Canadian Bank Notes*, 3rd edition, 524 pages.

With these publications, William K. Cross, his editorial staff and contributors have provided much needed additional coverage. I found it interesting to note that the 1998 coin catalogue, reflecting 52 editions (though not 52 years), paralleled the classic *Guide Book of United States Coins*, which then was "tied," with 52 editions.

In the latter months of 1954, James Elliott, Jr., and I worked independently on numismatic publications that would be the first to feature Government of Canada and Government of Newfoundland paper money. The problem faced by both of us was how to provide the illustrations that we deemed desirable in such a listing. The Bank of Canada and Department of Finance wouldn't give permission — citing restrictive provisions (sections 471 (b), 551) of Canada's Criminal Code. Elliott was more conservative than I, and published a detailed and informative paperback, wholly without illustrations. I allowed myself a reduced-size illustration of the face of each note. My thinking on the matter was influenced by Kernohan's "The History of Canada in Money" wall charts, which had been produced a few years before. I had understood that he had not been given permission for such educational illustrations, but had been told that the Department of Finance would not instigate action against him. Accordingly, I had gone ahead and published a catalogue on Canadian and Newfoundland government paper money issues, a 1955 issue date. As something of a precaution against possible seizure, I did keep most copies stored at my brother Herb's residence, in Mississauga. The only communication received from our central bank, however, was a purchase order for a copy. Elliot soon after released a supplement to his earlier publication, with large illustrations of face and back of all notes.

Much as the 1952 "Canadian coins and tokens" catalogue was a product of necessity, an idea whose time had more than come, a corresponding catalogue for the vast world of Canadian money (additional to government issues) was a real collector need 15 to 20 years subsequently. I set myself a deadline of the C.N.A. 1970 convention in Halifax, and the general feeling was that such a target couldn't be met.

The Canadian Paper Money Society was founded in 1964. From the start, there was agreement that such cataloguing was needed, and would be welcomed.

A 1971 catalogue revision, enlarged to 63 pages, covered commercial banks whose notes remain redeemable — freely speaking, chartered bank notes — and "broken banks" a classification which includes chartered banks which failed before Canada's note redemption fund was in place. Subsequent catalogue editions provided increased coverage, with 116 pages in the 26th edition of 1978.

What is most significant here, as with the "coin" and "token" ventures is the great assistance, continuing and freely given, of leading students and collectors; come but by no means all, acknowledged as "contributors" in successive editions.

One of the interesting developments in relation to the coin hobby that I have witnessed over the past half century has been the increasing number and distinct diversity of weekly, bi-weekly, monthly and other commercial publications directed to popular numismatics. Some such periodicals have rapidly come and gone, while others have stood the test of time and the vicissitudes of the hobby, to continue to make important contributions to the hobby to this date. With several of these I kept in close touch.

On location! In front of the former Bank of Upper Canada Building in downtown Toronto.

A new medium! Jim discovers that folding money comes over well on television, even in early black-and-white days. A September 1954 presentation on Toronto's CBLT that featured prominently

"A fair trade?" wondered Canadian Press. Jim sells a 1921 Canadian 50 cent coin (wrapped in a cellophane envelope) to G. R. L. Potter of Ottawa (left), purchasing — for $505 — on behalf of an unnamed collector. The year was 1955.

A graphic comparison. Jim displays line drawings of Canadian token classic's that give way to quality photography in later catalogue editions, and the outstanding engraving of traditional Canadian paper money.

Recognition of another sort has reflected Jim's lifelong involvement in golf.

Mint sets in plastic were considered a marked improvement over earlier cardboard packaging.

Television remains a particularly effective way of delivering a numismatic message. Jim at CBLT Toronto.

Business address, 80 Richmond Street East, Toronto, from October 1958 to August 1965.

Attractive window displays appeal to potential collectors in heavily traversed Yonge Street.

The Arcade Coin Store interior, 1963 - 1968, with Seymour Kazman, Harry Lumb, Frank Rose and Jim Charlton.

Numismatics Scrapbook Magazine was a quality monthly, put out by Hewitt Brothers, Lee and cliff, of Chicago, from 1934. It maintained a small format, 7 ¾" by 5 ¼," but was crammed full of ads, articles and new items. Its Canadian content was good. Something of a record was set with the 20 November 1958 issue totalling 292 pages, with an 18,800 press run. Ten years later, increased competition from newsprint papers was reflected in a decrease to 171 pages. *Coin World* took over and published *Numismatic Scrapbook*, from May 1968, and subsequently absorbed it into their weekly publication. Readers of *Numismatic Scrapbook* frequently were cautioned that anything too good to be true usually wasn't true; or, to reiterate, there was no Santa Claus in numismatics.

The Coin Collector was a newsprint tabloid with relatively early roots. As *The Philatelic Press*, it was launched, in Anamosa, Iowa, in 1935. Publishers were the Lawrence brothers — twin brothers Roy and Ray — and it was switched to a "coin paper" to reflect the editorial belief that there was more profit in coins, that stamps sold for "pennies."

The Coin Collector proudly proclaimed on its masthead, "The World's Greatest Paper for Coin and Stamp Collectors." The cover price was 25¢, a one-year subscription $2, two years $3, and foreign, $3 a year.

The first issue of *Numismatic News* came off the presses in October 1952. The publisher, then as now, was Chester Krause, of Iola, Wisconsin. Chet was raised on a farm, graduated from high school, and then worked with his father full-time in the family businesses of farming and construction. He saw service overseas in World War II, attaining the rank of Technician, 4th Grade.

It was Chet, the coin collector, who put out the one-sided 11" by 17" 'Introductory Issue,' a single sheet stating its purpose and introducing its publisher. *Numismatic News* would provide an opportunity for collectors, coast to coast, to trade and to correspond ... to buy and sell, and to exchange with fellow collectors who had duplicates and accumulations which they would gladly part to get coins needed for their collections. A simple idea for a publication, but an idea whose time had come.

Of the initial press run of about 650 copies, some 500 were folded and stuffed into envelopes on the dining room table and hand addressed by Chet's mother over the course of a weekend.

The second issue of *Numismatic News*, 3 November 1952, was expanded to four pages, with display and classified advertising and a few informational columns. The third and last of the three preliminary issues of unpaid circulation, the 1 December 1952 issue, consisted of six pages, although one page was promoting the paper.

With the fourth issue, 5 January 1953, also six pages, a $2 annual subscription charge was established, with low-cost display advertising and a free 20-word classified ad in each issue for subscribers.

Krause was convinced that a "trader" type newspaper filled with classified ads would be the backbone of any "collectable" hobby. That viewpoint was to extent to a range of other Krause publications over years that followed. I well remember reading early, monthly issues of *Numismatic News* on the streetcar from downtown Toronto to my east end residence. Although early paid circulation was much below expectations — only 40 for the issue of 5 January 1953 — Krause was disappointed but not discouraged. The 40 were send out, as were many sample copies, with gummed labels, the addressing machine not yet having been acquired.

Progress, admittedly, was slow, but by the beginning of its second year *Numismatic News* had increased in size to eight pages. A Canadian section was instituted in November 1953, with classified and display ads and, to start, a lengthy article on the history of Canadian currency.

An increase to 28 pages was to be noted in the November 1954 issue. Also, that issue was the first to include a photograph of a person. It was duly noted that the picture was not of the publisher, but, rather, of the Canadian numismatic collector, researcher, author and cataloguer, James E. Charlton! I was pictured with a backdrop of Canadian paper money, assembled for a Toronto television presentation.

In size, news coverage, editorial content, advertising and circulation, *Numismatic News* grew substantially over the years that followed. By 1964, issue size had reached 128 pages, with a circulation of 76,556 to paid subscribers and 7,325 to sell at coin shops. The press run has declined in recent years to perhaps 30,000.

Krause Publications had greatly expanded, and now produces hobby periodicals for such areas as coins, stamps, paper money, sports memorabilia, crafts, guns and hunting. In addition, numismatic, sports card and knife shows are being promoted.

One recent year, 1996, showed revenues of $63.4 million, and 395 Krause Publications employees.

Chet recently wrote me: "Krause Publications has continued to grow considerably, having about 55 different periodicals in the several fields in which they publish."

Chet Krause stepped aside as president in 1991, being succeeded (through 2000) by Cliff Mishler, a longtime member of the KP team.

Interest in collecting and in things Canadian. These can thrive in "retirement," as I can attest. Chet writes:

"I became quite interested in cars, trucks, tractors and gasoline engines, as well as World War II vehicles, through the years, and have about 200 pieces, as well as a sizable coin collection." He adds:

"You may well know that I bought one of John Pittman's 1936 dot cents at the last auction. I always wanted that coin, and John promised me one, but I guess he made lots of promises that were cut short upon his demise."

The Lawrence brothers, I do believe, were considered to be somewhat unconventional. One example was their own full back page advertisements — of coins and coin collectors supplies with a mail bid coin auction, and a "buy" ad. However, the periodical was apparently well received by dealers and collectors, and continued for over three decades. The 20 June 1963 Coin Collector, perhaps representatively, consisted of 40 pages, with many display ads, a page of classifieds, news items and articles, including extended reporting on the McDermott 1913 Liberty Head nickel — at that time, one of the more newsworthy of U.S. coins.

The Coin Collector was produced in Anamosa until 1966. Due to ill health, the Lawrence Brothers disposed of it to a Kewanee, Illinois publisher, who, in turn, sold it the next year to Krause Publications. It was merged with the Krause periodical, *The Coin Shopper*, renamed *The Coin Collector and Shopper*, and ultimately integrated into the *Numismatic News*.

With *The Coin Collector*, and with their coin and stock investments, the Lawrence Brothers did well financially, it would appear. In their wills they left funds to build an Anamosa community centre, which serves to perpetuate their names.

On reflection, my continuing commitment over the years to such numismatic writing as "coin" columns and features in hobby and general papers, may have had an outreach to established and new collectors that was second only to the much-needed catalogues. Of particular significance in this regard, I now feel, was my relationship of a good many years with the new and ambitious U.S.-based collector weekly, *Coin World*.

Few through that they — or anyone — could made a go of it back in 1960, a weekly coin paper, in terms either of news and feature content or of advertising and subscription revenue. Well, they did and still do, remarkably well, after over 2,000 weekly issues.

Coin World was inaugurated with a sample issue, Volume 1, Number 0, back in March 1960. In the industry, such a mock-up may be termed an "ashcan edition," and is used to show format, solicit business and attain copyright and mailing privileges. *Coin World*, Volume 1, Number 1, also a collector's item, came out on 21 April 1960. There has been a *Coin World* each week for, now, over 40 years.

Several months after the *Coin World* start-up, publisher J. Oliver Amos had me down to Sidney, Ohio, and received me most graciously at his home. Interest in Canadian numismatics had been evident among *Coin World*'s American readers, and from the beginning — "charter subscribers," such as myself — the paper also had a Canadian following. James Kelly's compilations of American coin market "trends" were popular with readers, and Amos proposed that I supply Canadian "trends." I did, from 23 January 1961. Trends were expanded to a Canadian Section of up to five pages, including news, features and pertinent advertising — commencing 10 May 1963 under *Coin World* editor Margo Russell. I prepared and edited the Canadian Section through 8 October 1969 when, seeking nominal retirement, I was succeeded by my friend and business associate, Frank Rose. On Frank's death in 1983, I resumed the *Coin World* commitment from 26 October 1983 through 7 November 1990.

You are aware, of course, of the great boom in collector interest in the Sixties. Such growth was more than paralleled by *Coin World* paid circulation. Beth Deisher, the current *Coin World* editor, tells me that paid circulation peaked at an incredible 175,670 on 10 March 1965.

As, so may years after, I leaf through full-page photocopies of such Canadian Sections, headlines bring those early years into sharp focus. In newspaper work, as you perhaps know, the writer does not always get to pick the headlines, but the following seem faithful to what I know I had to say:

"Cut-Off May Convention Topic," 20 January 1965.

"Market for Sets Remains Bullish," 27 January 1965.

"Set Fiasco Brings Bitter Fruit," 3 February 1965.

"Profit-Taking Sags in Proof-Likes," 12 May 1965.

"Early P-L Cutoff Plea Rejected," 1 September 1965.

"Teletype Demise Reflects Interest Shift," 16 November 1966.

"Banner Year for Canadian Collectors," 21 January 1967.

Those were the days!

Such material, I'm pleased to learn, does remain accessible. Libraries of the American Numismatic Association and American Numismatic Society do have archival microfilms of *Coin World* issues — from Volume 1, Number 1.

Canadian coin dealers were paying a substantial premium for ads in such U.S. coin publications as *Numismatic News* and *Coin World*, a large proportion of whose readers had little or no developed interest in Canadian coins. The obvious answer was to produce a separate Canadian paper, and Chet Krause set out to do just that.

The highly successful Iola, Wisconsin publisher established *Canada Coin News* in 1963, and opened a Toronto editorial office. His choice for the resident editor was Cale B. Jarvis, then coin columnist for Toronto's *Globe and Mail*, a director of the Toronto Coin and Stamp Exhibition, and an officer in the Canadian Professional Numismatic Guild. The new tabloid was to publish bi-weekly, with printing in Port Washington, Wisconsin. The inaugural issue was dated 3 June 1963, and Krause dispatched, in all, five issues, of up to 32 pages.

Problems with the post office and customers, paperwork, delays in deliveries and an estimated monthly loss exceeding $10,000 led Krause to turn over publication completely to Jarvis. By January 1964, *Canada Coin News* was putting out 36-page issues, with a circulation nearing 36,000.

Canada Coin News, like its U.S. counterparts, was experiencing decline in circulation and advertising revenues. Jarvis, from 1966, expanded the coverage of the paper, and changed the name to *Canada Coin, Stamp, Antique News*. He sold the publication in 1969, and died in 1980. Subsequent owners changed the name to *Canadian Coin News*, and launched separate periodicals directed to the stamp and antique markets.

Coin World takes a bow with the Number 0 issue of a "coin" weekly that has published over 2,000 issues to date.

A major trust company in downtown Toronto features Jim's promotional display in support of the 1962 TOREX event.

Numismatics goes on — poolside in Miami. Jim, with John Newman (far left) and Fred Samuels of Montreal, John Ford of New York, Hy Lipson and Manny Abravanel of Montreal at a Sixties F.U.N. event.

Jim joins John J. Pittman, left, A.N.A. and C.N.A. past president and outstanding "Canadian" collector, in reflecting upon a three-case "coin" display.

Frank Rose, Toronto professional, with Mayor Phillips of Toronto, and John J. Pittman, at TOREX, 1962.

An elaborate set blends the visual and the aural on an early Canadian Broadcasting Corporation television production.

Jim (left), with Mintmaster Norval Parker, at TOREX, 1963.

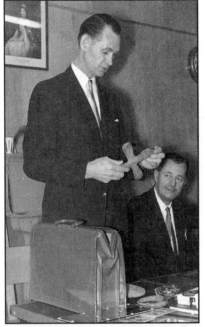

Brockville, Ontario, Coin Club features Jim as banquet speaker on 8 October 1963.

Mary and Jim, in a Toronto newspaper photo following an unsuccessful armed robbery attempt.

A dealer's dealer. Al Rosen (left) presents Jim with honorary membership in the Professional Numismatic Guild of Canada.

1959 STANDARD CATALOGUE

OF

CANADIAN & NEWFOUNDLAND

COINS, TOKENS

AND

FRACTIONAL CURRENCY

7th Edition

BY J. E. CHARLTON

Over 370 Illustrations, Valuations, Mint Reports and other information

Published By

CANADA COIN EXCHANGE
BOX 35, TERMINAL A
TORONTO, CANADA

PRINTED IN CANADA

*1959 Standard Catalogue of Canadian & Newfoundland Coins,
Tokens and Fractional Currency, 7th Edition*

5.

The Canadian Numismatic Scene

A year ago, many people thought the peak had been
reached when in the Canada Coin Exchange sale of March
31, 1951, an uncirculated 1921 50 cents brought $200 and an
uncirculated 1889 10 cents brought $67.

Sheldon S. Carroll
(Cited, Reference 15)

The story of numismatics in Canada really begins in
1862, the time of the founding of the Numismatic Society of
Montreal. The group, in 1866, became the Antiquarian and
Numismatic Society of Montreal, and commenced publication
of a periodical that today is one of the most prized items of
Canadian numismatic literature. The importance of the
Society was recognized in 1895 when it became the official
custodian of one of Canada's most historic buildings, the
Chateau de Ramezay (Scott 245, in philatelic perspective),
constructed in 1704 for the governor of New France.

The Chateau was formally opened as a museum of
Canadian antiquities and historical memorabilia in 1896, by
Wilson Smith, mayor of Montreal, the trust being formally
accepted by the president of the Antiquarian and Numismatic
Society, Judge Baby. Many noted numismatists were present
on this historic occasion, including R. W. McLachlan, whose
outstanding collection later was acquired by the museum to
form the backbone of the numismatic display. Among the
Chateau's noted curators was L. A. Renaud, who could
identify on sight — by Breton numbers — any of the 47
bouquet sous, and Fred Bowman, the engineer and scholarly
researcher. Unfortunately, some of the better material no
longer is in the Museum. Much was taken in a robbery
[Reference 49], and other pieces have been transferred to the
Bank of Canada collection in Ottawa, where an even greater
number of people should be able to view them.

This early period was in some respects a golden age of
Canadian numismatics — a time when such as Breton,
Leroux, Boucher, Hart, Wilson, Sandham, McLachlan, and
Courteau could and did distinguish themselves. These names
are familiar to collectors of Canada's colonial tokens [more
recent references: 23, 47].

We do know that a "coin club" functioned in Ottawa in the early 1890s, but evidently it was short-lived, with no data as to officers or activities currently available. Fittingly, it is best remembered by a token, Breton 825.

Tokens dominated this formative and important period of Canadian numismatics. The death of Courteau in the 1930s brought the interval to a close. With the Depression and World War II, there was little activity in Canadian numismatics until after 1945.

Nineteen fifty was a historic year for Canadian numismatics, with the national body, the Canadian Numismatic Association, being established. The association was an outgrowth of the Ottawa Coin Club, which had been organized in 1948. In my opinion, the association's founding and initial success also can be attributed to one of Canada's most knowledgeable numismatists having been the right man in the right place at the right time, and being the founding president. This was one of several major contributions of Sheldon Carroll to the advancement of Canadian numismatics in the last 50 years. Another was the planning and development of the central bank's numismatic collection.

J. Douglas Ferguson for many years was rightly regarded as the "dean" of Canadian numismatics. He possessed a wealth of numismatic knowledge, and was recognized for this both in Canada and the U.S. Although a highly successful businessman with many demands on his time, he always seemed to find time to answer inquiries and to encourage collecting. His collections of paper money, medals, coins and tokens were outstanding, and he was most generous in disposing of them to coin and medal museums.

Fred Bowman was a specialist, researcher and cataloguer of Canadian tokens, including the bouquet sous, province of Ontario and Quebec tokens, proof coins and decimal coinage of Canada and Newfoundland.

Guy R. L. Potter, an early C.N.A. president, was a dedicated Ottawa-area numismatist and prolific numismatic writer.

There are so many others from the early days. A random, necessarily incomplete, list would include officers and members of the Ottawa Coin Club, Toronto Coin Club and Canadian A.N.A. members. Norman B. Mason of Toronto was a frequent contributor to *The Numismatist*, as was Leslie Hill of New Westminster. John J. Pittman attended Toronto Coin Club meetings and C.N.A. conventions. He was the only president of both A.N.A. and C.N.A. Neil Carmichael operated several coin and stamp stores in Toronto. Milton Ritter was a dealer in stamps and coins, but his favourite area was paper money. He had a second floor office at the eastern end of the old Yonge Street Arcade. His business was known as Rose Stamps, and, as I recall, he was not an easy man to do business with. Bert Peddie was one of the most active collectors in the early days of the Toronto Coin Club, along with such as Bob Robillard, Norm Mason, Jack Sharpe, Sam Snider and Harry Roseborough.

Wayte Raymond's *Coins and Tokens of Canada*, 1947, was the only catalogue on Canadian coins in 1951. This was a great help, but even after four years, was outdated. Examples were an 1889 10¢, listed at $1.25, Unc, with one have brought $67 in a 1951 auction; also, a 1921 50¢, Unc, listed at $3 but receiving a $200 top bid in my 1951 auction. An interesting follow through is that a 1921 50¢, Unc, brought $3,000 at the 1958 C.N.A. convention auction in Ottawa, and a duplicate 1889 10¢, realized $3,000 at the 1964 Halifax convention.

After actively buying and selling coins since 1948 and handling four mail auction sales, I decided that it was time to produce a current Canadian catalogue. Fred Bowman and other numismatic students assisted with the 1952 (first) edition Charlton catalogue, and with subsequent revisions. The 2001 55th edition will very likely set the record for continuous issues of such a numismatic publication. As I have said, I was editor for the first 30 editions, 1952 through 1980; then Bill Cross took over from the 31st edition to date.

As Member No. 9 of the Toronto Coin Club, I had a close relationship with some other early members. Prior to 1953, the members met in private homes, and we enjoyed fellowship and refreshments, and shared numismatic knowledge. I remember on one occasion being at the home of G. N. Robillard, a past president, when we experimented in removing tarnish from a silver dollar by placing it in an aluminum pan, with baking soda and hot water. The tarnish was supposed to transfer from the coin to the pan. It was our first and last time for such an operation.

Although meetings had begun in 1936, Robillard had been named founding president in 1939. He was present at the 25th Anniversary meeting at the Royal York Hotel, 22 April 1961, and spoke briefly at the dinner.

Another Toronto Coin Club early member, Jack L. Sharpe, had had a nice home on St. Clair Avenue East, with a special room for his numismatic library and collection. A few of his bank notes were framed on the walls. He held a senior position, prior to retirement. His widow had me sell his collection by auction some years later.

Norman B. Mason had been a bachelor until well on in life, and had had ample time for a range of numismatic activities. Indeed, he was perhaps the most active of Toronto Coin Club members, and served as Canadian district representative for the American Numismatic Association. His reports from Canada appeared frequently in the *Numismatist*, the A.N.A. monthly publication, and he attended a number of the American annual conventions. He can be seen in group photos taken at such gatherings.

Mason had been employed by a large insurance company. He had married after his retirement, I believe it was, and had died a few years later. His widow had me handle the marketing of his collection.

Mason was among the first to recognize the rarity of Canada's 1921 5¢ piece, and had corresponded with the Master of the Mint, seeking insights into the reason for its scarcity. He left with his collection copies of articles he had written for various publications, numerous clippings from numismatic journals and papers, auction sale reports and a considerable file of collector and dealer correspondence. Although unknown to many of our present collector generation, Mason, in his lifetime, had made a significant contribution to Canadian numismatics.

Bert Peddie had been one of the early and long time members of the Toronto club, and his specialty was paper money. A prized possession was a Bank of Hamilton $5 note of 1922. In his listing, the U.S. auctioneer had said that the bill "might be negotiable," which would seem to have discouraged bidders less knowledgeable than Peddie. Peddie's bid of about face value had obtained him the scarce, redeemable note.

Bert had introduced me to a collector friend, Hector Mayes, who, like himself, had lived in West Toronto. Mayes helped me to complete my first date sets of Canadian large cents and large nickels. This had been something of a challenge, and I'd looked upon it as my first real accomplishment as a collector. Mayes also showed me his impressive and well-organized collection. He had housed it in a former upright phonograph cabinet, with trays, with recessed openings for coins, and descriptive labels. This had been conveniently located in the living room.

In retrospect, I credit Hector Mayes and other early members of the Toronto Coin Club for changing my direction and ambition from that of a cigar box coin accumulator to a numismatist.

Other early Toronto members included William Williams, J. Bruce Parker, Ted Parsons, John Sunden, Bill Morley, Fred Armstrong, Robert Hather, Peter Favro, Ernie Roseborough; plus such early post-war members as Sam Snider, Allan Townshend and myself.

Early out-of-town visitors were Peter Seaby, J. Douglas Ferguson, Guy Potter, Sheldon S. Carroll and John J. Pittman — who was a member.

That it was possible, with limited financial resources, to acquire such an inventory of Canadian coins, tokens and paper money, between 1948 and 1950, continues to amaze me, on reflection at this late date. Yet, substantial price lists had their start in 1949, and mail auction sales in 1950, to provide outlets for surplus material. Further, such sales results helped to establish current values, for the Standard Catalogue, from its launch in 1952.

The 31 March 1951 sales was the one that set records with top bids of $200 for the 1921 50¢ piece, Unc; $67 for the 1889 10¢, Unc; and $51 for the 1921 5¢ piece, abt F. While such pieces were quite a surprise at the time, they are — in a different sense — almost unbelievable today.

There was other such activity.

Fred Kraemer, a collector in Western Canada, disposed of his collection in a mail bid auction on 31 October 1949. There were, in all, 6,762 lots, but few rarities.

Frank J. Katen was perhaps the most active U.S. dealer in Canadian coins, providing auctions and itemized price lists in the 1947-1950 interval.

"Distributor of Coin & Stamp Collectors Supplies": sales representative Ron Mancey, with the Charlton van. License plate collectors? — that's a 1963 Ontario commercial tag.

One key to business success is the building of a strong team. Jim with his staff in 1965.

Coin groups, after 1950, were well established in centres other than Toronto and Ottawa. The Manitoba Coin Club, led by officers (seated from left) H. C. Taylor, J. W. Astwood, Ed Vincent, and W. King was an active club

Toronto leaders. The group that guided a coin club of exceptional longevity: Standing: Jeff Snider, John S. Wilkinson, Harvey Farrow, Mrs. Reta Frampton, Miss Frances Doane, Mr. Marvin Kay, Seated: Mr. Alex Monroe, John K. Curtis, president, Mrs. Nola Banky, Mrs. Louise Graham, H. A. Craig

"Canada Coin Exchange" presents three familiar faces on the bourse floor: Jim, Mary and Frank Rose.

Nick Gerbinski and Somer James (left to right, standing behind counter) operated Regency Coin and Stamp Co. (Western) Ltd. The firm produced interesting catalogues, and important reprints of such as Breton, Leroux, Courteau, Wood and McLauchlan.

Active promoters of the hobby in the late Sixties, Fred Jewett, Allan Fargeon, John S. Wilkinson and, (seated) Louise Graham, Mrs. Wilkinson and Mary Charlton.

Kenneth Gaver and Mrs. Gaver, highly respected Montreal-area dealers, take their Collectors' Research to the 1966 A.N.A. bourse. The couple's frequent, collector-oriented Bulletins proved to be both readable and informative.

Several such major U.S. dealers as Wayte Raymond, Max Mehl, Stacks, Elder and Schulman, had pre-1950 auction sales that included Canadian material. They, and Canadian dealers, continued such activities in the years that followed.

Some of the better coins to have turned up in Canada during this formative period originated in England. An auction catalogue from Glendenings of London proves revealing. There were some real buys at that time. One auction lot lists 1935 and 1936 Canadian silver dollars, then lists proof sets of 1911 and 1921. The price realized was, I see, 5 pounds and five shillings — 5 guineas, they might have said. Figuring about $5 for the pound and about 20 cents for the shilling, you'd come up with a price of, say, $26. Also, I see, listed, a Newfoundland 1880 $2 ("200 cents") gold piece, which sold for 5 pounds.

With 1953, new coinage for Queen Elizabeth II and a generally growing interest in Canada and its coins, resulted in unprecedented demand for mint-issue coin sets. Regrettably, the condition of offered coins deteriorated to that of bag uncirculated pieces, much inferior to sets of 1950 to 1952. Sheldon Carroll, as an active C.N.A. Ottawa-based member, approached the Master of the Mint about this, and the result was a promise to do whatever was possible to improve the quality of coin sets.

During the program of the C.N.A. Ottawa annual meeting, a Mint visit was scheduled, and we were able to purchase coin sets in white card holders. These proved to be far superior to the regular 1953 coin sets, and the descriptive term "proof-like" was unofficially adopted — for these, and for similar quality sets which became the regular issue in 1954 and following years.

A good friend, Dr. F. S. Epps of Homer, Michigan, had suggested the descriptive term, and it was used publicly in a Canada Coin Exchange mail suction that November: a set realized $15.50 in that sale. There was some criticism of the term "proof-like," but it became widely accepted, even for coins of other countries — though not by our mint.

Dr. Epps also may be remembered for inventing and marketing what he called "Koin Tains," holders which afforded good protection for individual coins.

The Toronto Coin Club was to host C.N.A.'s first national convention the next year — at the King Edward Hotel, in August 1954. Peter Seaby of London, England, was banquet speaker. Canada Coin Exchange had a 700-lot numismatic auction, which realized $5,819.81.

Auction highlights included the following Canadian items:

1858 large cent, Unc, $13; 10¢, 1871H, Unc, $10.25; 20¢, 1858, Unc, $9.50; 25¢, 1870, Unc, $7.25; 1945 silver dollar, brilliant proof, $18.50; 1948 silver dollar, brilliant proof, $17; 1914 $5, gold, Unc, $29; 1914 $10, gold, Unc, $42.25; $5 and $10, gold, set of six, Unc, $215.

The early Sixties — through January 1965 — was a time of wild speculation, in Canadian proof-like sets and brilliant uncirculated rolls and bags. Everyone seemed anxious to buy. Big profits were promised by some dealers, while others guaranteed against loss. The Royal Canadian Mint put on three shifts, and couldn't keep up with demand. Dealers joined teletype circuits, 34 dealers in one case (see Appendix G). Tons of coins were offered at coin shows. In my 6 January 1965 *Coin World* column, I warned collectors of the obvious danger. That column had been written early in December. On the night of 31 December 1964, a large crowd gathered outside the main Ottawa post office — with suitcases full of orders for "1965" proof-like sets. The orders would be posted at 12 midnight, in conformity to the rule that the Mint would accept no order postmarked before 1 January. Another rule imposed a limit of five sets per order. This resulted in speculators placing multiple orders, as by using names of members of various clubs. When Mint doors opened on 2 January, carloads of orders were delivered by the Post Office, orders for an estimated 6 million sets. It was decided that the best thing to do would be to accept orders for about 2 million sets, considered to be the Mint's annual capacity, and to return all other orders. Many of us who had been buying sets for years had our orders returned unopened — rubber stamped on the outside, "Quota Filled: Return to Sender."

All in all, it was a speculator's dream, as some had multiple orders accepted, and sold "futures" at up to $12.50

each. I paid $8.00 to get sets for my regular customers. Finally, on 31 January, following complaints that reached to Parliament Hill, the Minister of Finance directed the Mint to accept all orders, regardless of how long it took to deliver. This wholly unsettled the market for 1965 proof-like sets, and other sets, and bags and rolls went down in sympathy.

"Tried to Corner Market: Coin Speculators' Bankruptcy Called Boon to Collectors," the *Ottawa Journal* headlined in the interval to follow (Reference 13). A number of dealers went bankrupt. Coin clubs lost members, and the largest such club in Canada went out of existence. This was the Metropolitan Coin Club in Toronto. At the height of its prosperity, with hundreds of members, I had asked an officer about its educational program. He said: "Our members are interested in the auction and bourse, buying and selling coins." (See also References 27, 30, 31.)

At a St. Petersburg, Florida, coin show, a woman approached me for advice on Canada's 1965 "Type 4" dollar coins. She had a quantity of rolls which she had purchased at $100 each, and they then were selling at $200. I suggested that she sell, and take the profit. She was offended, declaring that she wanted to buy more, and to make more money.

Collectors and dealers who were not active numismatically in the early Sixties are right to wonder why BU Canadian cents of 1941, 1942 and 1944 are scarcer and priced higher than those of other dates between 1937 and 1947. This, despite higher mintages for the three years than the average yearly production of the other dates of the 1937-1947 interval.

Coin hoards? Yes, and with a story that reflects the turbulence of the early-Sixties numismatic period.

During the summer of 1961, shoppers at the T. Eaton Co. Winnipeg department store were, perhaps, pleasantly surprised to receive BU Canadian cents dated 1937 in their change. Some astute customers, realizing that the cents had to have premium value, went to other cashiers, requesting and receiving such "change." They then crossed the street to a conveniently located coin store, to cash in on their windfall. Catalogue value at the time was $3.00 for a BU 1937 cent. The coin store owner sought the Eaton manager, hoping to strike a deal for any remaining 1937 coins. The manager declined, but in investigating, stumbled on the mother lode.

The 8th floor of the store had had a cash cage in which were stored perhaps 300 bags of cents, for use as needed by store cashiers. The bags were piled high, and some lower bags had been there for many years. One day, however, an employee had taken a bag from the bottom of the pile, an original mint-sealed bag of 1937 cents. These cents had been distributed to various cashiers, in normal fashion.

The store manager, on learning of the significance of the "1937" find, had had an inventory made of all such bags. Veteran coin dealer Nick Gerbinski of Winnipeg has shared with me some relevant facts and figures.

Approximately 20,000 BU cents of each of the following years had reposed in the vault: 1937, 1938, 1939, 1940, 1943, 1945, 1946, 1949 and 1950. Only about 2,000 each of 1941, 1942 and 1944 were located, however, plus a few of 1947, and none of 1948. As well, there were a fair quantity of King George V cents from circulation, about six rolls each of the key dates 1922, 1923, 1924 and 1925, plus 25 rolls of common dates.

Eaton's decided to sell all the King George VI BU cents as one lot. The circulated key dates of King George V cents were advertised in a Winnipeg newspaper at about 65% of catalogue value, while the common dates were offered by the roll.

Regency Coins of Winnipeg entered into discussions with Eatons, resulting in the sale of the BU cents, for $20,000, to Regency; to Ray Hobin, a coin dealer from Stitsville, Ontario; and to a local investor. Gerbinski, in charge of Canadian coins at Regency, kept their share for stock. Hobin took the balance to Los Angeles, and sold the lot to a California investor, for $50,000.

At that time, 1962, Canadian coins were a "hot" commodity; and Les Depoy, a one-time owner of the 1911 pattern dollar, was promoting investment clubs, each with ten physicians. For an investment of $10,000 each, the doctors each would receive a package of Canadian coins, consisting of the 1858 20¢, 1931-1936 50¢, 1948 10¢, 1942 and 1943 tombacs and 1926 nickels.

That same year, Gerbinski had a bourse table at a major Los Angeles show during which Depoy was promoting Canadian coins in a most unusual manner. He had ten men dressed in Royal Canadian Mounted Police uniforms, giving out free Canadian cents, and inviting everyone to an open house upstairs in the hotel, for free drinks and snacks. In one of the evening meetings with Depoy, Gerbinsky and Regency sold him $35,000 of the Winnipeg "investment coins." To replenish such stock, "buy" ads were placed in Canadian newspapers, coast to coast. Dealers in Eastern Canada were selling in the same Los Angeles market. During the 1962 coin show, one doctor had told Gerbinski that he had bought 120 Newfoundland 1946-dated silver 5¢ pieces, and that he was prepared to take all that came into the market.

"Nothing comparable in Canada," from a numismatic perspective, I'm tempted to say. I refer to the Teletype Division, and associated sophisticated photographic services, at Van Horne Sales, an especially ambitious Sixties numismatic outlet high (38th floor) in the towers of Montreal's Place Ville Marie (Scott 688). A logical outgrowth of the Van Horne coin shop of Montrealers Fred Samuels and Harold Shaer, the upscale version was a salute to the Sixties coin boom, and a casualty when the bubble, perhaps inevitably, burst. I've the invitation of the Friday, February 12 official opening — that would have to have been 1965. Open were four teletype circuits: CANTEL (Coin Exchange Limited), P.C.D.E. (Professional Coin Dealers Exchange), U.S.C.E. (United States Coin Exchange) and I.T.C.S.E. (International Teletype Coin & Stamp Exchange). In addition, Closed Circuit Television, located in the board room, transmits full coverage of all happenings on the Cantel exchange, while a quotation board gives the latest prices on the most heavily traded coins. The heart of it all, four teletype machines located in a glass-enclosed teletype room, constantly supervised, keeping the investor in constant touch with the North American Market. Those *were* "interesting times."

Something of a turn-around came in the market for Canadian proof-like sets with the steep rise in the price of silver in 1979-1980. Silver reached a peak of nearly $50 an ounce, and common-date proof-like sets brought $26. Many silver coins from proof-like sets, along with common-date silver coins generally, ended up in the melting pot. The prices of silver and of late-issue silver proof-like sets, plummeted after the Hunt Brothers' failure to corner the market for silver. That, too, now is history.

6.

Personalities — and Great Friends — in Numismatics

Fraternal numismatics — in one essential dimension — is about people, both at collector and dealer level. I find my own memories of people an essential part of five decades and more of numismatic recollections.

The American Numismatic Association New York City convention in 1952 was my first major coin show and first bourse table, and it was exciting. Many others followed. In addition to American Numismatic Association annual conventions, United States gatherings included Florida United Numismatists, and Central States, California State, Michigan State, Empire State and Long Beach Associations. In Canada, all 47 Canadian Numismatic Associations, plus others from coast to coast, such as Torex shows in Toronto and the many conventions of the Ontario Numismatic Association.

I got to know a great number of leading dealers and numismatic hobbyists. Two of North America's best known dealers of the first half of the century were Wayte Raymond and Max Mehl. Both became fifty-year members of A.N.A. in the early Fifties, Raymond in 1952, Mehl in 1953. I much liked them both.

Raymond was a big man physically, while Mehl was small of stature. I had satisfactory business dealings with both, and with Canada's J. Douglas Ferguson, I helped in the pricing for Raymond's 1952 third (and final) edition of *Coins and Tokens of Canada*. Other dealers recalled include Sol Kaplan and Abe Kosoff, influential members of the Professional Numismatists Guild. Kosoff, with Ken Bressett, edited the A.N.A. Grading Standards for United States coins. I was one of the contributors.

While in New York City, I also met with Raymond in his Madison Avenue office. Raymond had been responsible for the only priced catalogue of the coins and tokens of Canada, first published in 1947. This effort was a great help to dealers and collectors of these series, but due to growing interest and competition for some previously unrecognized rarities, more frequent publication was desirable. Think: 1889 Canadian

Jim with Eva Adams, Director, United States Mint, at a Florida United Numismatists (F.U.N.) gathering, Miami Beach.

Canadian Imperial Bank of Commerce display of choice and rare notes from bank archives, 1967, finds Jim an interested Head Office visitor. The year marked the Canadian Bank of Commerce 100th birthday, as well as the nation's Centennial.

Dealer Loyd Carney, with Mrs. Carney, bring a rare London, Ontario note to the C.N.A. bourse.

Bob Willey places a bid at the 1968 Calgary C.N.A. Convention.

Residence and Club House at Broadmeadows Golf Course property. 1971 - 1974.

Jim, Mary and visitor at Broadmeadows, 1971.

Canadian Sculptors Elizabeth Wyn Wood, wife of Emanuel Hahn, and Dora de Pédery-Hunt.

Charles (Chuck) Martin, an early dealer and staunch supporter of the Sudbury Coin Club.

Numismatics long has been a male-dominated sphere of interest, so this group portrait of the hobby's ladies is well worth preserving. The descerning eye will spot Mary Charlton, to the upper left, and Louise Graham, C.N.A.'s first woman president, seated, second from the right.

10¢, Unc, $1.25 (quickly rose to $67); 1921 50¢, Unc, $3.00 (soon $200).

In the early Sixties, I would see Kaplan carry a blackboard around a bourse floor with "buy" and "sell" prices for U.S. proof sets. Those were the days!

Shotgun Slade III was a big man, and he carried a big gun, prominently visible at his bourse table.

Charles Wormser and John J. Ford of New Netherlands Coin Company had outstanding auctions of Canadian coins.

Hans Schulman maintained one of the best inventories of traditional ("primitive") and unusual money.

Jim Kelly of Dayton, Ohio was a leading U.S. dealer and auctioneer, and, until his death, editor of Coin World's trends (U.S. coins).

Grover Criswell was the big dealer in Confederate money, and maintained a money museum in St. Petersburg, Florida. His huge piece of Yap stone money was on exhibit at the Ripley Museum in St. Augustine until purchased for the Bank of Canada numismatic collection. I saw the piece in St. Augustine and Ottawa, and believe it weighed about 1.5 tons.

Mel Came was one of the big U.S. dealers in Canadian coins. However, in the early Fifties he declined to purchase a Bank of Canada $500 note, the 1935 issue. I had obtained three of them at face value, and — due to high face value and general lack of interest in paper money, had been unable to sell any of them at $525. They appeared to be a poor investment, so I used them to pay the printer for my coin catalogues. Today, such notes are rare, with perhaps 38 "outstanding," and the catalogue value for one with English text (fine condition) is $10,000.

Aubrey and Adeline Bebee were well established dealers, and published an excellent yearly catalogue of coins, paper money and accessories.

Copley Coin Company of Boston and Harold Whiteneck handled Canadian coins.

Frank Katen was possibly the first U.S. dealer to publish an itemized price list of Canadian coins, and one of the first to offer newly discovered 1936-dot 25¢ pieces.

Tatham Stamp and Coin Company issued a fine price list of numismatic and philatelic supplies, and handled large quantities of Canadian large cents and silver five cent pieces.

Indeed, Tatham for some years was my biggest and best customer for bulk quantities of Canadian large cents and silver five cent pieces. These I sold to the Tatham manager, H. E. MacIntosh, at very reasonable prices; and he, in turn, advertised them, with other Canadian coins, tokens and paper money, at very affordable levels.

As a lad of 16, MacIntosh had started collecting, with casual stamp sales while still in school. By the time he was 18, he had his own home-based operation, having added coins and supplies. This was 1929. Seven years later, "Tatham" had six to ten employees, and sales surpassing $70,000.

A *Coin Collectors Annual Catalogue of Coins, Tokens, Paper Money and Accessories* had been issued annually by Tatham since the Thirties. By the Fifties the catalogue had grown to 100 pages, and the company gave employment to 45.

The Tatham policy had been to offer coin collectors the greatest variety of high-grade accessories at low prices, and that policy undoubtedly contributed to the company's success.

The modest mark-up on Canadian coins that I supplied, no doubt influenced many Tatham customers to start in that field.

Another Tatham catalogue item that was of special interest to me for a number of years was the un-cut sheet of six Champlain and St. Lawrence Railway notes — offered in the 1948 catalogue for $5.00, but reduced to $3.95 in subsequent editions. Either it was a slow seller, or else there was a large inventory. I did help out by buying a few sheets.

MacIntosh was an innovator in selling coins, paper money and postage stamps "on approval."

Forty per cent of his later sales were in coins and bank notes, I understand.

The Tatham business ended in 1958, failing to survive its founder's untimely death at 47.

Neil Carmichael I first met in 1948. He had a stamp and coin counter in a barber shop at 198 Bay Street, in downtown Toronto. He later opened a store, also on Bay, near Front, and a book store on Front Street, between Bay and Yonge. His most successful outlet was at 31½ Bloor Street East (Subway Arcade), about 1954. On Saturday mornings, the store was so crowded with young people that, at intervals, they all would be evacuated by his assistant, Boris Meshenko, to permit entrance to others.

Carmichael and I had frequent transactions in numismatic material, and he had allowed me to display some of my mail auction lots in one of his stores, prior to having opened my own. Carmichael published a number of small catalogues on Canadian coins, tokens and paper money, and the coins of Great Britain; also, pamphlets on "funny money." In my opinion, Carmichael was more successful in business than in politics, where he supported the Social Credit movement.

One of the many interesting numismatists I have met at coins shows and conventions was Mr. McDermott. He was a pleasant, heavy-set man, from one of the Central States, I believe. His prize coin was one of the five known United States 1913 Liberty Head nickels. He kept it in a 2 x 2 plastic holder — for protection, as he frequently tossed it on the table, for anyone to see. He died in the mid-1960s, and his widow consigned the piece to Paramount Coin Company, to be sold at the 1967 A.N.A. Convention auction, in Miami Beach. The convention was held at the Americana Hotel, and I had a bourse table during the day, and in the evening joined the large crowd in the auction room. Jim Kelly was the auctioneer. After spirited bidding, the 1913 Liberty Head was sold to Aubrey Bebee, for $46,000. Possibly the most surprised person in the room was Bebee's wife, Adeline, who told me that she hadn't known that Aubrey was even going to bid on the coin.

Grover Criswell made quite a name for himself as a leading dealer in Confederate and Southern States paper money, and as an author of catalogues and other references on these fields. He also operated a money museum, which he closed after a burglary. Criswell it was who loaned the 7 ½ foot piece of Yap stone money to Ripley's Believe It or Not Museum in St. Augustine, Florida, the same piece which was sold to the Bank of Canada for its museum holdings.

Joseph Powers was an early member, number 152, of C.N.A. His full-page ads in *Numismatic Scrapbook Magazine* of coins to sell, and offers to buy, underlined his interests in things Canadian.

Hans Schulman, a leading U.S. dealer, sold through sales catalogues, at fixed prices, the Couteau collection of Canadain tokens, medals and numismatic publications, in the mid-Forties. Schulman also sold the Gibbs collection of odd, unusual and primitive money, from which I purchased sufficient to build two collections, the one which I sold to Canadian Imperial Bank of Commerce, and the one which I retained for exhibits and talks. The latter included a small example of Yap stone money.

James Kelly of Dayton, Ohio, was a well-known U.S. coin dealer, whose periodic bulletins contained coin news and, on occasion, exceptional coin offerings. Kelly was the founding editor of *Coin World*'s U.S. coin "Trends." I joined Kelly for the A.N.A.-C.N.A. joint convention auction in Detroit.

Maurice M. Gould was with Copley Coin Company back in the Fifties, when the firm was a strong source for Canadian coins. Gould became a syndicated newspaper columnist in later years, and relocated in Sepulveda, California.

Michael Kolman, Jr., of Federal Brand Enterprises Inc., of Cleveland, was a substantial and active dealer, with auctions particularly big business for his firm. A high point was his 1963 "Million Dollar Auction Sale," held at the Hotel Fountainebleau in Miami Beach, 3-7 January. I believe it to have been the first sale having a "million dollar" billing. However, the quality and quantity of featured material would compare favorably with the multi-million dollar sales that would follow.

Dominion of Canada $1 and $2 notes of 1870 — both serial 00001, position letter A, and HALIFAX backs — would have been of particular interest to Canadian "paper" enthusiasts. The notes were graded Fine, and bore at the left end the penned signature, "C. E. Ratchford."

The Bebees, from Omaha, were highly respected and successful coin dealers. They had been stamp dealers in Chicago, but made the switch to coins after their Nebraska move. They now are deceased; but most generously donated the 1913 Liberty Head nickel, an 1804 United States silver dollar, and rare United States bank notes, to the A.N.A. Money

Museum, where they can be seen at the Association's headquarters in Colorado Springs.

A gentleman of distinguished appearance one day visited the Canada Coin Exchange store on Toronto's Richmond Street East and said that he was interested in buying Newfoundland $2 gold coins. After examining a number of pieces, and agreeing on the price for several of them, he asked if I would accept his cheque. I hesitated momentarily, and he asked that, for verification, I call the Royal Bank of Canada main Toronto branch. This I did, and was promptly informed that John MacKay-Clements was a highly respected and responsible client of the bank.

This was the start of an excellent relationship. MacKay-Clements was a highly successful businessman, a philanthropist, a civic leader ... and numismatist. His collection of Canadian coins, tokens and paper money was one of the best. It included the "king" and "prince" of Canadian coins (the 1921 50¢ and silver 5¢), the 1911 pattern dollar, and a considerable quantity and range of rare and choice condition items.

MacKay-Clements was a frequent visitor, and exhibitor, at coin shows, and a contributor of numismatic writings. The eventual sale of his holdings, by Frank Rose at the 1976 Ontario Numismatic Association convention in Toronto, was one of the most important in years, with 2,550 lots.

A good numismatic friend for many years was Richard S. Yeoman of Whitman's Coin Supply Division. His family name was Yeo. Dick and I were closely associated in the coin supply business, and in the authoring and publishing of the *Standard Catalogue of Canadian Coins, Tokens and Paper Money*, 1960 to 1970 editions, and the Charlton-Willey *Standard Grading Guide to Canadian Decimal Coins*.

With the growing interest in Canadian coin collecting in the early Fifties, there was a demand for coin and paper money holders, and these I had purchased in small quantities from U.S. dealers to meet the needs of my customers. In connection with an A.N.A. National Coin Week in the 1950s, I had had an exhibit of coins, in Whitman coin folders, in the T. Eaton Company store window, in downtown Toronto. A store manager contacted me, and said that customers had wanted to know where they could purchase such folders. Of course, I had the answer; and this, and other Eaton stores, developed into good customers.

With increased sales, Canada Coin Exchange was to become the largest Whitman jobber for coin supplies in Canada. Whenever possible, however, Canadian supply sources were made use of.

In 1959, Yeoman contacted me with a proposal for a new, expanded edition of the then 40-page Standard Canadian Catalogue. He considered that the U.S. represented a good potential market. If I would author it, Whitman would produce and market the catalogue. At that point, distribution of the Canadian catalogue remained quite modest, and I realized that Whitman had the facilities, experience and market potential, that I couldn't match — so I agreed. The result was a 1960 edition of 128 pages, blue cloth bound, and with the addition of Government of Canada and Newfoundland paper money, and individual (rather than group) illustrations of the coins and tokens. Although token likenesses had been line drawings, it became possible, through assistance of the American Numismatic Society, to incorporate actual photos in subsequent editions. The new catalogue format was deemed an outstanding improvement. Such progress, together with rapidly growing interest both in coin collecting and in the fields of Canadian decimal coinage and Canadian colonial tokens, resulted in markedly increased catalogue sales, with press runs of 100,000 copies or more.

One production quirk did continue to impose a limitation, however. While Whitman was to publish 11 annual editions, the Canadian catalogue, in practice, was restricted to 128 pages. A press could only handle a sheet equal to 128 pages, using printing on front and back. Other Whitman catalogues, at the time, were similarly restricted to 128 pages or a multiple of 128 pages: the Handbook of United States Coins was 128 pages, the Guide Book of United States Coins was 256 pages, and the Catalogue of Modern World Coins was 512 pages.

Yeoman's able assistant for a number of years was Kenneth Bressett. Ken, also, was a good friend, and made a name for himself as an author, numismatist and respeced past president of A.N.A.

Whitman and I parted company in 1971.

The Charlton Trophy for best Junior Exhibit is awarded to Sam Veffer at C.N.A.'s 1972 convention.

A start to retirement. Jim receives his A.N.A. 25 year Silver medal from A.N.A. president Virginia Culver in 1975. Jim recently was presented with his A.N.A. 50 year Gold medal.

Charlton business premises were in this commercal location at 92 Jarvis Street, Toronto, from August 1965 to July 1967.

A tradition is perpetuated. The Charlton enterprises after leaving Jim's hands.

That year, my enlarged, 200-page paper-back Canadian catalogue incorporated new material on redeemable paper money of chartered banks, and on other obsolete notes. This release was followed by yearly editions, increasing in size through a 1978 edition of 341 pages.

Bill Cross of The Charlton Press and Charlton International Publishing Inc., put out the 1974 and subsequent editions. Some content reorganization ensued. Tokens and paper money were deleted from the 1979 edition, marketed as *Charlton's Standard Catalogue of Canadian Coins*. With the 1980 (30th) edition, I retired as editor.

Of U. S. dealers active during early years of the past half century, I knew and did business with many.

Frank Katen, a C.N.A. member from 1950, was one of the more active in dealing and promoting Canadian coins. Katen featured Canada's 1921 silver five cents in his 1948 A.N.A. auction catalogue. Katen was one of the first dealers to direct attention to Canada's 1936 Dot 25¢, around 1949-50, and to the Newfoundland 1946 5¢, as mentioned by Sheldon Carroll in a 1950 C.N.A. *Bulletin.*

Harold Whiteneck of Court Coin Company, Boston, was a major dealer in Canadian coins, as evidenced by full-page advertising in *Numismatic Scrapbook Magazine*. He purchased late in 1958 the 1921 Canadian 50¢, for $3,100, that earlier that year had been auctioned for $30,000 at C.N.A. in Ottawa.

C. C. Shroyer, know to many of us as "Tim," was A.N.A president from 1961 to 1963, so held that post when the joint A.N.A.-C.N.A. convention was held in Detroit. Shroyer had served as an A.N.A. governor from 1951 to 1959, and was life member 211.

Harold Bergen, also an A.N.A. past president, was a gracious host during my visit and speaking engagement at Fullerton, California, 10 March 1979. The occasion, a most interesting one, was the 11th Annual Numismatic Educational Symposium — and invitational exhibits — of the California State Numismatic Association.

Melvin Came, of Dover, New Hampshire, and Key Largo, Florida, was one of the early dealers to feature Canadian coins and paper money, as well as U.S. and world coins. I do recall, though, how, in the early Fifties, he declined my offer of a 1935 Bank of Canada note, priced by me at only $525. There was little interest in Canadian notes, particularly higher denominations, in those days.

Charles Wormser and John Ford of New Netherlands Coin Company had a part of the 1952 A.N.A. convention auction, plus a number of their own auctions in the Fifties and Sixties. High grade Canadian items frequently were featured in their sales. In the sixties, John Ford was commissioned to market Le Chameau treasure (Reference 32).

John J. Pittman offered distinct leadership to organized numismatics in both the United States and Canada, and quite possibly attended more coin conventions and coin shows than anyone else. Even in later years, when in a wheelchair, he took part in such events as Florida United Numismatists shows of 1996 and 1997, where I spent time with him and with Gehring, his wife.

I represented C.N.A. at the January 1996 reception for John, and read a letter from C.N.A. president Yvon Marquis. Both John and Gehring expressed gratitude. In a sense it was a timely farewell. John passed away on 17 February 1996, hours short of his 83rd birthday.

Gehring I subsequently met with at the 1998 F.U.N. convention. She, her daughter Polly and I were at some of Bob Hendershott's centennial year celebrations. While clearly missing John, Gehring and Polly were giving thought to a planned trip to Australia.

Although my major business dealings involved the popular areas of Canadian numismatics, my interest was and is the historical and educational aspects of the field. Only once did I accept an invitation to speak on investing — or speculating — in coins. This was in the early 1960s when there was a mania for speculating in uncirculated rolls, mint sealed bags, and proof and proof-like sets and dollars. Harold B. Metcalf Sr. had a series of classes on "coin investments" at Purdue University, and he had asked me to speak on the investment potential of Canadian coins. Instead of recommending the material that then had mass-market popularity, I suggested that a more prudent investment would be in key date and better grade Canadian coins. I don't think that anyone who took that advice at that time lost money, while the BU rolls and bags of cents and nickels plummeted in numismatic worth. Fortunately, the bullion value of silver (which soared to $50 an ounce in 1979-80) saved some of the investment in silver coins.

While I find no suggestion that Metcalf had been other than honest and well intentioned, even carrying additional life insurance to protect his "partners" (speculative fellow-investors), his unexpected death provoked an estate and succession nightmare, according to contemporary reports (*Coin World*, 8 June 1966, quoting the *Indianapolis Star*).

Among my more interesting Sixties recollections are of visits to the studios of two of Canada's foremost sculptors, Elizabeth Wynn Wood and Dora de Pédery-Hunt. I was privileged to view some of their "work in progress," as well as completed work. After my 1965 visit to the Wynn Wood studio, I sold for her some uncirculated silver dollars and proof 1939 10¢ and 25¢ pieces, as listed in our August 1965 Subscribers' Bulletin. Her late husband, Emanuel Hahn, had been the designer of those three coin reverses.

As a relevant point of interest, there has been controversy regarding the identity of the ship on Canada's 10¢ piece — as to whether it represents the racing and fishing schooner *Bluenose* or is a composite model. The Hahn's daughter Mrs. Kennefor Brown of Fort William asserted that the *Bluenose* indeed had been the model — based on what she had seen in the studio at the time that her father had been working on the design.

One of the prominent coin dealers in the Montreal area was Louis Goldsmith. Goldsmith operated a retail store on Sherbrooke Street, near Decarie. He also was active on the teletype circuit.

At the Canadian Numismatic Association convention auction in Montreal in 1965, Goldsmith and Colby Tracy of Fredericton Junction, N.B., were bidding on a coin, each with a raised hand, while engaged in animated conversation. Due to apparent difficulty in hearing, their faces were close to each other, and it was obvious that, unknowingly, they were bidding against each other. After other floor bidding had ceased, being alerted to the situation ... one hand went down.

Tracy, a former railroad employee, was one of my good customers for a number of years, passing away in the late 1960s. Goldsmith I counted among several Montreal-area wholesale accounts. He was an interesting conversationalist on the teletype circuit.

"THESE BILLS SHOULD GO GOOD AT REGINA – FRESH OFF THE PRESS!"

Jim heads to the C.N.A. in Regina. Cartoon by a young admirer in anticipation of the 1959 convention

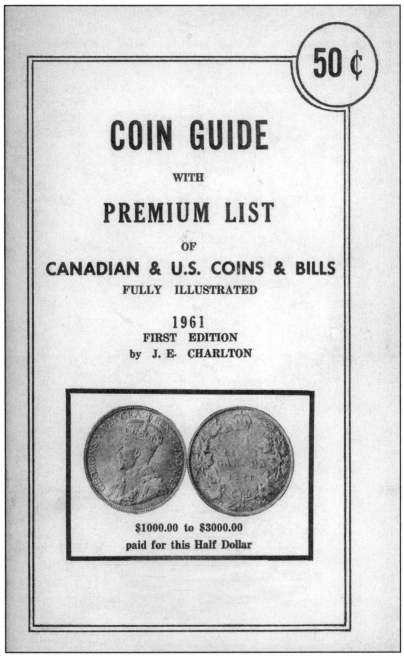

COIN GUIDE

WITH

PREMIUM LIST

OF

CANADIAN & U.S. COINS & BILLS

FULLY ILLUSTRATED

1961
FIRST EDITION
by J. E. CHARLTON

$1000.00 to $3000.00
paid for this Half Dollar

50 ¢

Coin Guide with Premium List of Canadian & U.S. Coins & Bills, First Edition (1961)

7.

Interests ... and Adventures

As a young collector I was quite proud of my complete date sets of Canadian large and small cents and large nickels, plus a variety of Canadian colonial tokens, obsolete United States minor coins and my one Roman coin. Soon after starting the Canada coin business in 1949, I realized that it was not possible for me to be both a coin collector and a dealer — for two reasons. I was not able financially to support both, and it would be unfair to my customers to compete with them for coins and other numismatic items that came on the market.

It occurred to me that if I was going to collect anything linked to numismatics, it would need to be inexpensive and in lesser demand. I solved the problem by choosing unusual and primitive money. There were few collectors and few dealers, and for the most part pieces were quite reasonable. Hans Schulman, a prominent New York coin dealer, issued a catalogue and price list of the material, and it proved possible to assemble a collection with purchases from him and other sources of supply. Howard Gibbs had possibly the best private collection of unusual and primitive money, and I believe that he supplied Schulman. I was one of the few who had built such a collection. John Rejitko was another. It made an interesting display for television appearances, coin shows and speaking engagements. School teachers were grateful for classroom visits by members of the coin club, where the connection of money with history became evident. The Canadian Bank of Commerce was impressed with the collection, and persuaded me to rent it out for a year. It was used to attract visitors to branch openings. The popularity was such that the bank was reluctant to return it after the year, so purchased the collection. I learned afterwards that the bank made five or six separate displays, to reach more branches. It was time for me to put together another collection of unusual and primitive money. This I did, and supplemented with further historically interesting coins and notes.

As a numismatic dealer and auctioneer in the early 1950s, I felt a particular interest for Canada's paper money — and its distinct collecting challenges — with notes of one large former institution, the Bank of British North America,

Jim (right) with Jim Haxby and Frank Rose at TOREX in October 1975. Haxby is known for his numismatic research and writing. Rose became a well-established numismatic dealer and auctioneer.

Dealer Bill Cross (left) became Canada's foremost publisher of numismatic and collectibles references. With Cross are Quebec collector Roger Beaulieu (centre) and Terry Brown, Head of Charlton International Publishing Inc.

Jim with C.A.N.D. Honourary Lifemember Al Bliman, talking "coins" at Toronto's Calico Public School, May 1978.

Jim speaks for Canada at the 1978 Metropolitan Washington Numismatic Association Educational Forum — with fellow-panelists Frank Katen (left), Gover C. Criswell, and Stella B. Hackel, U.S. Mint Director.

proving quite scarce or rare. (The Bank, uniquely, had been directed from London, England, since being established in 1836; when, in World War I, such arrangements had proven disadvantageous, it had been merged with Bank of Montreal in 1918. Notes remain redeemable.) It was, accordingly, a pleasant surprise when, in 1956, I learned of a hoard, at a Toronto bank, being readied for shipment to Ottawa and destruction. I rescued the lot, and offered selections in the 1957 C.N.A. convention auction, and in subsequent years, so that as many collectors as possible could possess the previously unobtainable notes. Seven of these bills were in the C.N.A. 1958 convention auction, with particulars and prices realized as follows:

Domiciled Toronto, $1, 1856, F-VF, $73.00; Undomiciled, $5, 1886, AU but small tear, $50.00; $5, 1886, F-VF, $45.00; $5, 1886, VG, $20.00; $5, 1911, Fine, $35.00; $10, 1877, G-VG, $43.00; $10, 1889, abt Fine, $50.00.

An interesting and rewarding aspect of numismatic investigation is the connection or relationship of coins, tokens, medals, paper money and such, with historic events and famous people. As a teenager, it was my privilege to be an eye witness, even a minor participant, in an historic event, featuring royalty, which had occurred in Toronto. The year was 1927; the place, the Princes' Gates, at the Canadian National Exhibition, eastern entrance.

The Gates had been constructed that year to commemorate the 60th anniversary of Canadian Confederation, and were designed in the traditional architectural form, the Triumphal Arch, which was surmounted by a statue of the Goddess of Winged Victory. The figure was cast in concrete, standing on the prow of a ship, surrounded by mythological sea horses, and it weighed an estimated 16,000 pounds.

On 30 August 1927, the Princes' Gate was officially opened by H.R.H. Edward, Prince of Wales, and his brother, Prince George. A parade of veterans from across Canada, sponsored by the Canadian Legion and militia units, lined Lakeshore Boulevard to greet the Princes, and followed the Royal Party through the Gates and to the grandstand. They then took their place in the Guard of Honour for the final review. At the time, I was a teenager, and a young recruit in the No. 1 Batallion of the Canadian Machine Gun Corps.

Needless to say, it was quite a thrill for me to be there. The Prince of Wales, in his address, siad that he had just experienced another wonderful trip across the continent and back, and was pleased to see so many veterans. His speech was unusual in that it was entirely his own composition and typewritten by himself. Afterwards, he autographed his notes and gave them to the Canadian Legion's acting president.

Nothing lasts forever in this life. After 60 years, the statue of Winged Victory atop the Triumphal Arch was in bad shape, and even dangerous condition. Exposure to the elements had led to deterioration, inwardly and outwardly, to the 16,000 pound cement statue. Removal was necessary for public safety. It would be impossible to repair the damage, so it was decided to make an exact copy in a lighter material. In 1987, a new Winged Victory, weighing 1,500 pounds, was hoisted into place, a beautiful cream coloured resin epoxy finish to protect it from water and sunlight. On the eve of the 109th Canadian National Exhibition, the new statue was unveiled, with a spectacular fireworks display. Inside the Princes' Gates, a plaque commemorates the official openeing and review by the Prince of Wales, back in 1927.

In 1987, on their 60th anniversary, it was again my privilege to walk through the historic Gates.

A portrait of the Prince of Wales as a child was featured on Imperial Bank of Canada $5 notes of 1902, 1906 and 1910. A likeness in the uniform of the Welsh Guards is to be found on the Merchants Bank of Canada $5 of 1919, and also on the many variaties of Dominion of Canada, 1923-dated, $2 note. These frequently collected note varieties involve seal colours and signature combinations. Finally, a portrait of the Prince of Wales (in military uniform) appears on the orange $5 of the Bank of Canada's 1935-dated first Issue, such notes being circulated in both English and French texts.

The 1919 date on the Merchants Bank note is significant, the note having been issued to mark the Prince's first visit to Canada and first return transcontinental trip. The date of the 1923 legal tender $2, June 23, also is significant, being in recognition of the Prince's 29th birthday, on that day, and which would coincide with his visit to Ottawa. However, a production delay prevented note release before November. The note remained Canada's basic $2 denomination until Dominion of Canada notes were succeded by the smaller size Bank of Canada first issue of 1935.

"Join the Navy and see the world." Great traditional advice and, as well, a familiar saying from my early years. Not specifically the advice that I followed, however, I seem to have reinterpreted it as, "Join the Canadian and American Numismatic Associations, and see your continent!" Since signing up for those two fine organizations half a century ago, I have travelled east and west, south and north — for coin show, conventions, speaking engagements and numismatic business, in both Canada and the United States. This travel has included visits to many major cities, and the seeing and experiencing of more of both countries than otherwise would have been the case.

Mary, my wife, and I had an overseas trip in 1978. Though unrelated to the coin business, it did serve as a reminder that numismatics knows no boundaries. On our visit to Rome, at the Sistine Chapel in the Vatican, a coin collector from Belleville, Ontario, recognized and greeted me.

Our travels took us to the Roman fortress city of York, the Emperor Hadrian's wall, the Parthenon and the Pyramids. While in Isreal, we visited Masada, the Dead Sea and the Wailing Wall. We journeyed down the road from Jerusalem to Jerico, seeing on the way the ruins of the 20th century Inn of the Good Samaritan. While some of these sites do have a direct relation to numismatics, other simply are historically interesting, and these appealed to us, too.

Closer to home, my first visit to Houston, Texas, was in 1975, the A.N.A. Convention, at the Shamrock Hotel. Like most others, I had been hearing a great deal about the Lone Star State, especially how big everything Texan was. However, I was somewhat amused when it was suggested to me that the hotel swimming pool was large enough for water skiing. I said I would have to see this to believe it, feeling that the claim was stretching things a bit too much. After supper that first night, I did watch water skiing on the hotel pool.

You may, in this regard, have heard the story of the Englishman, the Frenchman, the Italian and the Texan. It seems that the Texan was boasting of the magnitude of everything in Texas.

The Englishman asked, "Have you anything to equal Buckingham Palace?"

"Yes," was the reply. "We have hotels with more rooms."

The Frenchman asked, "Have you anything to match the Eiffel Tower?"

The Texan answered, "Why, yes. We have oil derricks which are higher."

Finally, the Italian asked, "But do you have anything the equivalent of Mount Vesuvius?"

The Texan hesitated for a moment, then said:

"No, we haven't. But our Dallas Fire Department would soon extinguish it."

The 1960 Canadian Numismatic Association Sherbrooke convention I have several reasons for remembering. It was decided to make the trip of about 400 miles from Toronto by car. We left Toronto in the afternoon, and, realizing that it would be late in the day when we reached Montreal, I asked my assistant to nap on the way, and later to take over the driving. Possibly he was too nervous of my driving to take a nap. On reaching Montreal, therefore, I decided to continue as driver to Sherbrooke, as he then seemed more tired than I.

The well-known English dealer, Peter Seaby of London, had a Canadian 1911 silver dollar pattern that he offered to sell for $15,000. This was the first time that any of us in Sherbrooke had seen the piece. Even to John J. Pittman, the asking price seemed high. The piece had changed hands a number of times since then, and recently sold for $1,000,000.

One of my more disconcerting experiences occurred at the Sherbrooke gathering. After a successful evening auction session, and delivery of much of the material to successful floor bidders, I noticed that the cheques and bills were missing from the cash box. Mary, my wife, had retired early, and woke to hear the distressing news. "Oh," she responded, "I have them under my pillow ... for safekeeping."

A sad note at the Sherbrooke convention was the theft of coins from the car trunk of Charles Kirk, Toronto dealer.

The fact that a good number of Canadian collectors now possess Canada's $5 "train note" in its early "no seal" variety can be traced back — nearly half a century back — to the minor civil servant who allowed himself an astute detour on the way to the bank. The federal employee had been dispatched to "cash in" a crisp bundle of 100 of the old Dominion notes, and his detour was to Jim Kelly's Ottawa Stamps and Coins. Kelly rewarded him appropriately, and the "no seal" 1912 $5 is significantly more accessible today than otherwise would have been the case. I learned about this in 1955.

On one visit to the Toronto main branch of Bank of Montreal in 1959, I was offered a good quantity of the Bank of Montreal $10 final "large" issue of 1931, all in uncirculated condition. The note was in little demand, being considered at that time a "recent issue." Nevertheless, I took a few dozen, and it took years to market them.

One day in 1963, I believe it was, a gentleman who had been aware of me as a numismatic professional took me to his bank and showed me a dozen uncirculated 1935 Bank of Canada $25 notes and two original uncirculated rolls — in their cardboard tubes — of the corresponding 1935-dated commemorative silver dollar. This was in the safety deposit area of Bank of Montreal's Toronto main branch. Quite naturally, I asked if he was interested in selling them. No, he had said, though he was a stockbroker and not a collector as such, he had bought them, and was keeping them, as "something different." A year or so later, I had a call from dealer Lloyd Carney, asking if I'd be interested in buying twelve $25 notes, uncirculated, and two BU rolls of 1935 silver dollars. I was interested, and bought them. The stockbroker had died, I learned. His widow had sold the notes and coins to Carney.

A couple from a mid-western Ontario town visited my office on a Saturday morning — in, I believe, 1968. With them they brought a particularly large quantity — perhaps 500 — of the Bank of Canada $10 note of 1937, Gordon-Towers signatures. They were interested in getting rid of the lot, but I was hesitant to buy such a quantity, with a rather limited potential market. However, I decided to take the lot — many were uncirculated — paid a fair price, and kept about a hundred. The balance, actually, were to serve as a part payment on a property in Magnetewan.

I do have my full share of "coin" related experiences having to do with air travel. One of the more improbable involved getting to Indianapolis to be present at an "investment" seminar at Purdue University. I had taken Air

Canada from Toronto to Chicago, then I would transfer to a small North Central plane to Indianapolis. A stop was made at Lafayette. After some delay, the passengers were informed that there was engine trouble, that they should leave the plane with their carry-on luggage, then proceed to the waiting room. Another plane would be arriving shortly, on which we would complete our trip to Indianapolis.

After perhaps 30 minutes further delay, we were informed that no relief plane was available, and that we would have to go by car to Indianapolis.

To my surprise, the Airport Manager turned to me, and asked whether I had a driver's license. When I said yes, he requested me to drive a car, with the four other passengers, to the airport in Indianapolis.

I'd never been to Indianapolis, and had no idea of the way, I informed him.

He produced a road map, and the keys to a car, and sent us on our way.

With some assistance from back seat drivers, the five of us did arrive safely; and I could recommend collector coins, rather than bags and rolls, to those gathered at Purdue.

One of my early visits to Los Angeles was for the 1958 A.N.A. convention, which was most worthwhile. Afterwards, I took a night flight to Chicago, where I was to board Air Canada for Toronto. A dense fog ruled out landing at Chicago, however, and we were diverted to Milwaukee. Shortly thereafter, the captain directed passengers to fasten seat belts in preparation for landing. It was evident that the plane was rapidly descending. I had a window seat — and, with visibility still nil, I was somewhat concerned, and remained so, until a few hundred feet above the Milwaukee Airport, the runways appeared. After landing, passengers were shuttled by bus to Chicago Airport. The fog remained a problem, and my Air Canada flight, and others, were delayed. We were provided with breakfast and lunch. It was near supper hour when I learned that our Toronto flight would be canceled. The next scheduled departure would be the following morning. I did have the option of taking an overnight train to Toronto, and that I chose to do. I arrived at noon, more than 24 hours later than my original schedule.

Jim along with Serge Laramee presenting Rolland Labisssionére with the Paul LeBlanc Trophy at the
Numismatic and Philatelic Association of Boucherville, Inc., 8th Annual Exhibition, in 1978.

The kind of crowd that one hopes for! Jim, as C.N.A. president, participated in this
Boucherville, Quebec coin show in 1978.

Business — and pleasure.
Jim autographing *Standard Catalogues* for
1973.

Richmond Hill, radio station, as Jim "talks
coins" and fields questions for Coin Week
Canada.

Harry Eisenhauer (left) and John G. Humphries compare topics prior to a Canadian Paper
Money Society Presentation at "Interpam" in Toronto 1981.

Frederick C. Jewett brought to my attention a particularly large hoard of notes of the historic Westmorland Bank of New Brunswick that had become available 40 years ago. I was able to purchase several hundred of these notes.

Jewett had been president of the Toronto Coin Club in 1957-1958, and was a leading paper money collector for many years. He held a senior position with Bank of Nova Scotia at its Toronto main branch.

Jewett had outstanding collections of notes of the Bank of New Brunswick, which had merged with Bank of Nova Scotia, and of the Westmorland Bank, I understand.

The "mix" of Westmorland notes that I acquired was interesting in several ways. Of the bank's first issue, $1, $2 and $4 notes of 1854-1859, with thin paper, black face designs, plain backs and no face tints, there were only a few. Of the later issue, $1, $2 and $5 notes, 1861-dated, there was a good mix. The face designs, black with green tint, were quite attractive, as were the ornate blue backs. All notes in the hoard gave evidence of having been in circulation, but condition tended to VG and better. Prior to appearance of this hoard, Westmorland Bank notes had been quite scarce, and they are by no means common today.

Several other note hoards of varying size came to light over the years, and were marketed, with little or no related publicity.

Bundles of uncirculated Molsons Bank $5 and $10 notes of that bank's 1922 issue came into the hands of Montreal dealer Philip Spier. I first heard of them in 1955, and believe that he had 100 of each.

C.N.A.'s 1959 convention auction included a particularly large quantity of Canadian notes. The notes derived from a major hoard which had come to light in Selkirk, a small town near Hamilton. An elderly man had died, and the family had discovered an estimated $10,000 in old Dominion of Canada large size notes, chartered bank notes (mostly large size) and Bank of Canada 1935 issue notes. The family took the money to the bank, and were delighted to receive full face value. The notes were forwarded to the bank's Toronto main office, and were being made ready for shipment to Ottawa and the firey furnace. However, I had a relationship with the manager of the silver cage, and he phoned to see if I was interested.

I hurried over to the bank, and was amazed by the amount and diversity of the money. In retrospect, I feel that I should have bought it all, but this had been 40 years ago. At that time there had been relatively few collectors of paper money. Also, at auctions, one bidder might represent a syndicate of perhaps five or six collectors, which could result in little competitive bidding, and relatively low prices. I think this is evident when I compare 1959 bids with those of later sales which had more collectors competing.

Giving consideration both to rarity and condition, I chose what I felt to be the best of the notes. The choicest went into the C.N.A. auction (as Consignment 'S'), and the rest became inventory, being marketed over a number of years. My friendly banker had helped with a loan, and hundreds of old notes had been saved.

1970 Standard Catalogue of Canadian Coins Tokens and Paper Money, Eighteenth Edition

8.

Florida ... and Relative Retirement

Magnetawan, Florida: A hole in one was scored by
James E. Charlton on the 9th, 118 yard hole at the
Broadmeadows Golf Course on Tuesday, September 11. Mr.
Charlton was playing in a foursome with his wife Mary, club
members Paul and Shirley Nelson. The ace enabled Mr.
Charlton to set a course record of 32 for the nine holes, one
under par.

Clipping from 1973

All in all, it was perhaps not surprising for me, in my early days, to have been fascinated by such as the Horatio Alger book stories. Without consciously having emulated young Horatio, I had left the family homestead at 22, and had made my way, independently, in Ontario's rugged North Country. I didn't find fame or fortune; but I found Mary, my wife, a greater treasure.

My retirement was delayed and restructured, but never forgotten. In July 1967, the supply part of the business, and the building at 92 Jarvis Street, were sold to J. A. Forbes. The Canada Coin Exchange business, at that point, was relocated to 6 Adelaide Street East, Room 509.

In 1968, the Arcade Coin Store was sold to Frank Rose, its successful manager since its inception in 1963. Canada Coin Exchange and its inventory were disposed of in 1969. Under new owners, Canada Coin Exchange undertook the Canadian Paper Money Society, Toronto Dominion Centre, auction, February 28 - March 1, 1970.

My first visit to Florida was in 1962 ... for the Florida United Numismatists (F.U.N.) convention at the Cherry Plaza Hotel in Orlando. At that time, before Disney World, Orlando was a small city, with no major airport. It was necessary to fly to Tampa, then to take a bus to Orlando. This I did, and was somewhat surprised by the cool early-January temperature in the low 30s. However, that was better that Toronto, and with bright sunshine, the next day was quite pleasant. Just outside the hotel was a park-like setting, with a body of water, a small lake, with a concrete walk around it, an ideal place to relax.

The following year, F.U.N. met at the Fountainebleau Hotel in Miami Beach, only a short distance from the airport. At the time, 1963, the Fountainebleau had been an outstanding luxury hotel, possibly the finest in the area, with spa, pool and oceanfront beach, and, of course, excellent rooms and meals. Fortunately, our rooms had been discounted 50 per cent.

The 1964 F.U.N. gathering was at the Jack Tar Hotel, in Clearwater. This was a popular hotel and location, and four of the F.U.N. conventions were held there. Sol Kaplan had thought that it would be a novel idea to hold a Professional Numismatists Guild membership meeting on an excursion boat ... while cruising. Unfortunately, it was a cold and blustery morning, and it proved to be a short meeting and cruise.

It was back to Miami Beach in 1965, and another luxury hotel, the Deauville, with facilities similar to those at the Fountainebleau.

The Soreno in St. Petersburg, an older hotel, was the F.U.N. site for 1966. Although, for me, business was nothing special, the mid-winter breaks from Toronto weather were reason — or excuse — to attend.

More recently, I have met many currently prominent numismatists and dealers at such as the 1998 F.U.N. get-together at Orlando's Orange County Convention Center. I was particularly glad to see and talk with F.U.N.'s president emeritus, Robert Hendershott, and to attend some of his 100th year celebrations. Hendershott is F.U.N. Life Member 2, and has been a mainstay of the Florida organization from the early days. It was noteworthy to see Bob patrolling the bourse floor, as he has done for decades, greeting visitors ... and without even the use of a cane.

Subsequent to the sale of Canada Coin Exchange on 1 May 1969, I had one final auction, at the C.N.A. Convention, Royal York Hotel, 28-30 August 1969. I find it interesting to reflect that my first C.N.A. auction also had been in Toronto, 23-24 August 1954.

After the 1969 auction and the settling of related accounts, my "retirement" really commenced. However, I never wholly divorced myself from numismatics. As a young man, my hope had been to retire early. To help to make this possible, I had purchased an insurance annuity policy — back in 1936 — which would guarantee, from age 55, for life, monthly payments of $80. I didn't realize that our cost of living would be much higher in 1966, or that Mary and I would be a substantial business — actually, a combination of three. However, in addition to my ambition of early retirement, I sensed that the business was consuming too much of my time, and leaving little for my wife and son. Although a bit delayed, I was able to attain my goal in 1969, having sold my business interests in three parts, in 1967, 1968 and 1969.

Soon after retiring from Canadian numismatic commitments, I purchased 330 acres of land at Magnetewan, north of Huntsville, complete with a nine-hole golf course and a big house. For a couple of years, a most interesting experience! Another Florida adventure was the investment in an eight-room apartment house in Boca Raton. The biggest such undertaking, however, was the investment in a 21 acre orange grove. This may not sound all that exciting, but it proved to be quite an experience, with unexpected developments. A Florida family had owned considerable acreage, on Lake Huntley, for many years. In passing from one generation to the next, the land had had some portions sold. What remained was a bit over 20 acres of undeveloped prime lakefront property. Unfortunately, included in portions sold had been the land connection to the highway, and owners of the land declined to sell a required portion. We did make a deal! I was to have 2.386 acres of waterfront property. I had 18 condo units built. The owner, Philip Moore, and his family were given in exchange, access to a mutual road serving his 56 homesites and our 18 condo units — so 74 residences were possible from the trade.

The Charlton Standard Catalogue of Canadian Paper Money, First Edition (1980)

9.

After Five Decades

To and from the Canadian Numismatic Association's 50th anniversary convention in Ottawa, the event with which we close these reflections, Mary and I travelled by train. Actually, it was mostly by train. We drove out car to the Guildwood station, just east of Toronto, and boarded the Ottawa train. Our return was simply the reverse procedure. It may have taken a bit longer, but was more relaxing, avoiding airport hassle, car parking problems and general inconvenience.

As a 50 year member, I received a framed 50 year certificate, a 50 year lapel pin, a copy of the C.N.A. history, a medal portraying Sheldon Carroll and a souvenir note.

A distinctive exhibit which certainly caused me to reflect was Dan Goslin's large display, perhaps six cases, of the coin catalogues which I edited, 1952 through 1980; the auction catalogues, 1954 through 1969; and the supply catalogues.

One of my less expected numismatic adventures in my early retirement years was being called as an "expert witness" in one of the country's longest — and highest profile — court cases. The trial concerned the division, and handling, or numismatic treasure — $700,000 in gold and silver coin — from Le Chameau, the 18th century French pay ship which had been wrecked and sunk off Cape Breton.

The "find" made headlines on 5 April 1966, with subsequent coverage in the likes of *Time, Argosy* and *Life*. "Three young skin-divers said they had recovered an estimated $700,000 in gold and silver from the wreck of an 18th-century French pay ship," said the Canadian Press, Louisbourg dispatch. Headlined *Canadian Coin News*, "Sunken Wreck Yields $700,000, Three Canadian Divers Say." Alex Storm, leader of the group, subsequently wrote a book on the initial adventure, *Canada's Treasure Hunt* (1968). Two days after announcement of the "find," however, Storm's former partners initiated court action to prevent him selling or disposing of the treasure — claiming that it belonged to them. The case went to the Supreme Court of Canada, culminating five years of litigation.

A foremost promoter of Canadian Numismatics at home and abroad, Jérome Remick, like Jim a 50 year C.N.A. member, joins Jim at an O.N.A. event.

Choosing our illustrations. Jim at the Ontario Numismatic Association's Ottawa gathering, 1999.

C.N.A. 2000 Tom Kennedy (left) with Stan Clute (right) presenting Jim with his work "A half century of advancement in Numismatics."

Continuing support for Canadian Numismatics. Jim at the International Coin Fair, Oakville, Ontario, September 2000.

Somewhat to my surprise, then, while vacationing in Florida, I received a telephone call from a Halifax lawyer. This had been January 1973. Alex Storm again was the defendent in a court case over the Le Chameau treasure, this time relating to the sale and distribution of the coins. I was asked to appear as a so-called numismatic expert, on behalf of the defendent.

My thoughts on the treasure and the trials are well detailed, in Toronto and North York coin club bulletins and in the *Canadian Numismatic Journal*, September 1976 (Reference 32).

I often reflect on developments in Canadian numismatics since World War II, an interval in which I was active and now can view with a sense of perspective. Those of us most involved are understandably impressed with developments and with the contributions of so many numismatic students, past and present, and of publications, associations and such.

Those early postwar years know but one catalogue on Canada's coins and tokens, and that was the Wayte Raymond. Now, we have a number, plus works on paper money, trade dollars, medals and much more. Of late, William K. Cross of Charlton Press is Canada's leading publisher of reference catalogues on the country's numismatics, and on other 20th century collectables, with more than 30 titles and editions released to date.

The Canadian Numismatic Association, established in 1950, has held yearly conventions since 1954, at cities across Canada, with a joint convention with the American Numismatic Association in Detroit in 1962. Such conventions represented a unique opportunity to "get together," and the bourse and the public coin auctions were highlights of such occasions. Other such numismatic auctions were held in connection with a range of meetings and shows. These include Torex, Monex, the Toronto International Coin Fair, Ontario Numismatic Association conventions, Canadian Association of Numismatic Dealers and Canadian Paper Money Society Gatherings, and many provincial or local groups, and commercial and dealer-sponsored events.

Such auctions serve a useful purpose in establishing current values, and aid in making available, distributing and marketing numismatic material. To attend or participate in such an event can be an educational, sometimes exciting, experience.

In such contexts, I have had some quite memorable experiences. As one instance, at C.N.A.'s Hamilton convention in 1961, I was the auctioneer for the first such public sale of a Canadian 1936 Dot Cent. The value estimate: $2,000. With his hand raised like the Statue of Liberty, John Jay Pittman stood until no one any longer challenged his bid: $3,400. Harvey Brubacker of Preston, the consignor, had obtained the piece from G. R. L. Potter of Ottawa, for $900, I understand. A follow-up: At the David Akers Numismatics, Inc., Stuart, Florida, sale of 21 October 1997, the winning auction bid for one of the Pittman 1936 Dot Cents was $121,000 — that's U.S. — including a 10 per cent buyers fee. I understand that the piece was purchased by a Canadian collector.

Then, there was the Paramount International Coin Corporation auction, 11 August 1967, where James Kelly sold the J. W. McDermott U.S. 1913 Liberty Head Nickel for $46,000.

The Frank Rose auction of the renowned McKay-Clements Numismatic Collection was of particular interest to me. I had assisted the consignor in building the collection, and had had a close relationship with him. The sale was a highlight of the O.N.A. 14th Annual Convention at Toronto's Westbury Hotel. Included were many outstanding rarities in Canadian coins, tokens and paper money; plus, foreign coins. The catalogue is worthy of a place on any numismatic shelf.

Of particular interest in the 2,550 lot auction were three prestige pieces, the so-called "Prince of Canadian Coins" (the 1921 silver 5¢), "King of Canadian Coins" (the 1921 50¢), and "Emperor of Canadian Coins" (the 1911 pattern silver dollar). This auction was the first and only time that the three pieces have been featured together. In choice uncirculated, the 5¢ brought $5,200, and the 50¢, $21,000. After excited bidding in a crowded auction room, the pattern dollar went for $110,000 — to Douglas Robins, a well-known U.S. dealer in Canadian coins. This was the coin that first appeared at the C.N.A. 1961 Sherbrooke convention, with no takers at $15,000. It sold at the following years joint A.N.A.-C.N.A. convention, changing hands several times before finding its place in the McKay-Clements collection — at a price of perhaps $55,000 to $60,000, in cash and trade. Subsequent to the purchase by Robins, the pattern changed hands several times, the last reported sale price being $1,000,000.

It was a thrilling experience for many of us, including the media, in a standing-room-only auction session, for the Torex Auction of Jeffrey Hoare, 25 October 1997. For sale to the highest bidder were the World War II medals of Colonel John McCrae, the author of "In Flanders Fields." (The further numismatic relevance of the back of Canada's Issue of 2001 $10 note, we hardly could have anticipated). The value estimate for the lot was $20,000. After the amazing interval of sustained bidding, the successful bid was $400,000. The added buyers charge and taxes would bring that to close to a half million dollars. I found it gratifying to hear of the successful bidder's decision to donate the medals to a museum for public display.

The auction scene continues as quite central to the hobby. Since his first sale at O.N.A's 1977 convention auction, Charles Moore has become a leading auctioneer. Two of his recent sales have been Bank of Canada related auctions of 13 November 1999 and 18 November 2000. The first sale comprised primarily the central banks unissued "specimen" notes (1935 through 1979-dated issued) and low-number notes of 1969-1979 — notes deemed surplus to the bank's continuing needs. The second sale comprised primarily "specimen" notes from the Birds of Canada issue, and "low serials" of such later issues. The bank is committed, I understand, that the few such notes held back from these auctions will not be available for future sale.

With closing of Eaton's stores in the late Nineties — who could have foreseen that eventuality? — some coin and stamp dealers were having to relocate to new premises. I am reminded of the early Fifties, the time at which I got Eaton's started handling coins and coin supplies in their downtown Toronto store. This followed, and resulted from, a Coin Week exhibit in one of their store windows. Their customers showed keen interest, particularly in such as Whitman coin folders and numismatic catalogues. Concessions also were opened in some of their other stores.

The image of a coin dealer in the eyes of the public may vary according to the public's actual experiences in buying or selling. As has been related, it was so bad at mid-century, when I was starting out, that a leading national weekly refused my advertisement relating to coins because so many reader complaints had been received regarding coin dealers. The hobby has achieved some degree of respectability in the intervening years, and I know of no publication at present turning down coin advertisements. In fact, a number of papers have an established tradition of carrying coin columns.

Unlike most trades or professions, coin dealers are relatively free of government regulations. It also is possible to be a dealer without any special training, course of study, or even actual experience in numismatics.

Before obtaining my First Class Stationary Engineer's certificate, I was required to have ten years actual operating experience as an engineer, and then to pass an examination that took several days. However, as a coin dealer — a numismatic professional — I graduated, as did many others, from the status of a collector without any course or examination. My feeling is that despite great advances in numismatics, there has been relative neglect in the educational program for both collectors and dealers.

Many of us have learned by a trial and error method, but this can be very expensive training. Also, it affords little protection for the inexperienced collector or the general public, who may be unintentionally victimized by errors in grading, classification or pricing of coins.

Much has happened since first I penned those thoughts, some 35 years ago. I suggested courses. I advocated that local, regional and national gatherings provide, in their programs, time for more structured numismatic education. Some good things currently are being done — workshops, correspondence courses, seminars. For example, the C.N.A.'s Canadian numismatic correspondence course — inexpensive, well run — is accessible to all desiring to pursue such numismatic self-education. Beyond our borders, A.N.A. has been furthering such efforts for some decades, often with a particular slant toward the young. A.N.A. also has had extended course offerings, with some scholarships available, at its college-campus Headquarters in Colorado Springs. A significant Canadian counterpart has been an ambitious full-day course, not necessarily restricted to correspondence course completers. A recent Canadian Numismatic Course circular gives a stated goal of "educating collectors about the beauty, historical and economic importance of Canadian coins, tokens, medals and paper money." With Paul Johnson as the able moderator, well qualified instructors would be presenting on Canadian coins and commemoratives, the coining process, Canadian paper money, Canadian tokens, collecting strategies, coin and paper preservation, and the grading of coins and tokens.

It does make you think.

What a leap forward from the release of a 34-page coin and token catalogue (Reference 23) being, for some, the numismatic happening of the year!

The manner and extent by which several numismatic items have increased in value can be of interest, even to those for whom grade and price are a most secondary consideration.

A 1936 Dot Cent, Unc, we see was sold by G. R. L Potter to Harvey Brubacker, in 1955, for $900. The same coin brought $3,400 at the C.N.A. 1961 Hamilton convention. Described as "gem specimen," such a piece sold for $110,000, in the 1997 David Akers Numismatics, Inc. sale of the John J. Pittman collection (Part One).

A Canadian 1921 50¢ piece, Unc, had a top bid of $200 in the Canada Coin Exchange mail auction of 31 March 1951. Such a piece, at the C.N.A. 1958 Ottawa convention auction, brought $3,000. Auctions by Bowers and Merena Inc. sold such a coin, from the Norweb collection, Mint State 67, on 15 November 1996, for $90,200; and another piece, MS 65, from the "Victoria" collection, 11-13 September 1989, for $110,000.

Myddelton tokens of 1796, in copper and silver, show similar, if less extreme, upward movement. The Canada Coin Exchange mail auction of 30 November 1950 included both copper and silver proofs. The copper realized $46; the silver, $40. The 1997 Akers auction (John J. Pittman, Part I) had a copper proof sell for $13,750. The Bowers and Merena "Frontenac" sale of 20-22 November 1991, saw a silver proof bring $4,070. (U.S. sale prices are in American dollars, and include the buyer's premium.)

After 50 years in numismatics it would not be possible to relate all the interesting experiences, but paramount and with gratitude I will always remember the social equality and camaraderie among collectors and dealers. It has been truly said, as we were reminded by Miguel Munoz at the C.N.A. Calgary banquet in 1975, that numismatics knows no boundaries. This applies equally to geography and to humanity.

It was my privilege and honour to do business with, and to associate with, people from all walks of life, trades and professions, and I usually had a feeling of personal relationship, which extended to correspondence. Some of these were: Fred Bowman, J. Douglas Ferguson, Sheldon S. Carroll, John J. Pittman. The unique contributions of these individuals, and of so many others, long will be remembered. For me, the help of these four with early editions of the *Standard Catalogue* was of great importance.

One of my early good numismatic friends in Toronto was Vincent G. Greene. Greene, who was C.N.A. president from 1956 to 1959, was also a noted philatelist. He had served as chairman of Capex in 1951 — the major Canadian stamp exhibition which was held in the old Automotive Building, located on the grounds of the Canadian National Exhibition.

Greene had been a military officer during World War II and numbered among his friends such business tycoons as E. P. Taylor, Colonel Phillips and Bud McDougald of Argus Corporation.

Greene was an insurance agent, with a second floor office on Victoria Street between Richmond and Adelaide streets, across from the rear entrance to Yonge Street Arcade. He seemed to enjoy having visitors during noon hours, and a small glass of wine would be available if desired. I would occasionally visit, and was rewarded with consignments for my auctions. There were three coins that I received which will always be remembered. In early 1951, Greene told me that he had two uncirculated 1889 10¢ pieces for auction. This surprised me, as I'd not handled that date in better than VG, and there was great demand even for the lower grade. I suggested that he check the date. He did so, and brought one of the Unc 1889 10¢ pieces for the 31 March 1951 mail auction sale. It was listed with an estimate of $30, and sold to John J. Pittman for $67. The other Unc 1889 10¢ was included in the C.N.A. 1964 Halifax convention auction, the estimate being $2,200. It sold to Allan Fargeon of Montreal for $3,300. It changed hands after his death, and the last record I have of it was its listing in a Montreal auction, with a $20,000 estimate.

In my opinion, the 1889 10¢ piece is possibly the rarest Canadian coin in uncirculated condition. The Pittman specimen was slated to be sold in Part Three of the Pittman Collection auction, by David Akers Numismatics, Inc., in 1999. It sold for U.S. $24,150.

In addition to those two 1889 10¢ pieces, Greene consigned to the 1958 Ottawa C.N.A. convention auction a BU 1921 50¢ piece. It was listed, I think for the first time, as "King of Canadian Coins." In choice Uncirculated, with an estimated value of $3,500, it sold for $3,000, and was sold again, to Harold Whiteneck, the next day. Whiteneck sold it at a later date.

Greene consigned other high quality coins and tokens to my auctions, including the Bateman collection of tokens.

Fred Jarret was one of Canada's leading philatelists of that time, and a close friend of Greene. Jarret consigned to me some rare medals, including the Fort Detroit, Chateauguay and Chrystlers Farm; also, foreign coins, and Indian arrowheads and other artifacts. Dust storms of the Thirties in Western Canada removed much top soil, exposing quantities of such items.

While wintering in Lake Worth, Florida, in 1960-70, we had a visit from Greene, with his friend, John A. ("Bud") McDougald, one of Canada's wealthiest men. They had come from McDougald's Palm Beach oceanfront mansion. Although McDougald had about anything that money could buy, including a Bayview estate and a barn for his collection of antique cars, he was troubled by a weak heart, and couldn't play golf. He died at a comparatively young age.

Colonel Phillips became interested in paper money, and had Greene help him to assemble a worthwhile collection by buying selected notes for him at our auctions. He, too, died, and his collection was purchased by the Canadian Bank of Commerce.

McDougald and Phillips had been large shareholders in Argus Corporation, and their widows sold out to Conrad Black and his brother, who gained control.

Vince Greene, in his later years, let a rather lonely life. His wife had spent many years, and eventually died, in a sanatorium in Guelph. Greene had continued to maintain his office after reaching age 90, but his hours were shortened, and his working days per week reduced. Finally, the office had to be vacated to allow building renovations. Greene died at about 94 years of age.

When Mrs. Greene had been able to go outside for a brief walk, she would visit a small nearby park. This, I understand, now is her memorial.

Why do we collect, you and I? At the Toronto Coin Club's 50th anniversary banquet in 1986, the keynote speaker was a psychiatrist, a Dr. Henry Fenigstein. I don't know whether any of us needed a psychiatrist, but I thought that he might relate some interesting case histories. Suddenly, he turned to me, and asked, "Mr. Charlton, why do you collect coins?" This was unexpected. I was not on a couch; and it was he who was supposed to be making a speech. However, I quickly gathered my thoughts.

My reply was, in essence, that I found in numismatics a fascinating and most interesting hobby — because of the connection between money and history; the record of civilizations and of people, places and events, and of the money associated with them.

A fair statement, I think.

On reflection, however, I do have a further — and concluding — thought:

"The best thing about numismatics is the numismatists," someone has sagely asserted. How true that is! We meet on common ground, regardless of age or of professional, political, financial or intellectual standing.

In these reminiscences, I've tried to share with you a few of the recalled highlights of a lifetime, and more than a few of the personalities that have meant much to me.

The Charlton Standard Catalogue

$12.95

1st Edition

of
Canadian Government
Paper Money

The Charlton Standard Catalogue of Canadian Government Paper Money,
First Edition (1984)

10.

In Conclusion

Here, I want to allow myself some, to me, important reflections and extensions, and to say some things that I'd been saving for insertion at this point.

Three Canadian numismatic legends of my lifetime are men to whom I wish to pay tribute. These three, need I say, are J. Douglas Ferguson, Fred Bowman and Sheldon S. Carroll. In addition to their varied commitments, their busy lives and non-numismatic responsibilities, they were most helpful to me, generously sharing their superior knowledge and giving encouragement. From the early days of the Canadian Numismatic Association, all three were among my best friends.

In that first of my catalogues, back in 1952, I acknowledged my appreciation of these three numismatic leaders, and they remained important contributors to subsequent yearly revisions.

The Canadian Numismatic Association is a legacy of Sheldon S. Carroll, as is the Bank of Canada Currency Museum.

The huge and outstanding lifetime collection of J. Douglas Ferguson — coins, tokens and paper money — in virtual entirety, was acquired by the Bank of Canada, and became the basis of the national collection. Doug's medals and military decorations went to the Riveredge Museum, in Calgary.

Articles and books on Canadian tokens by Fred Bowman remain classic references. Fred's early *Decimal Coinage of Canada and Newfoundland*, with permission, was a major contribution to early Charlton catalogues.

As photographs record, Mary, my wife, was of great help. She prepared price lists and mail auction catalogues at our residence — in those particularly early years. Some years as store manager followed. Later, Mary was a valued assistant at some convention auction sales, at bourses and in our Arcade store.

After five decades of such numismatic activity, I have many pleasant and grateful memories of people, places and events. This work is an honest effort to record these, for present — and, yes, future — "coin" hobbyists.

Harold Don Allen — so long an active numismatic popularizer, in North America and overseas — has undertaken, for me, to take my nondescript recordings, and to revise, correct and add to, as necessary, in preparation for publication.

Over the past 50 years, I've had 18 different residences in Canada, and those moves may have caused record keeping to suffer. At this point, the volume of pertinent material has been impressive. Don has willingly taken on a formidable task!

Present-day Canadian numismatics is characterized by a diversity of groups, each with its interests, its adherents, its priorities — but striving, more often than not, for a common cause. Let me recall some that have welcomed me, or interested me — and, as a consequence, made for a distinctly richer overall experience:

Canadian Numismatic Association, Numismatic Educational Services Association, J. Douglas Ferguson Foundation, Canadian Association of Numismatic Dealers, Canadian Numismatic Research Society, Canadian Paper Money Society, Canadian Association of Token Collectors and Canadian Association of Wooden Money Collectors.

And our fine regional, provincial and community groups.

We're much impressed by what we see — and read — at the more local level. The Ontario Numismatic Association, under John Regitko, puts out a comprehensive and most useful *Ontario Numismatist*. Don, a *membre à vie*, speaks most highly of bulletins of the Société Numismatique de Québec, a "city" club with remarkable outreach.

Then there are the U.S.-based groups and periodicals, in whose benefits we so readily can share.

And organizations that demonstrate that numismatics can be international — indeed truly worldwide — in scope.

Our publisher for this project, most fittingly, has been William K. Cross at The Charlton Press. Bill has taken what

I started, that slim paper catalogue of five decades ago, and has expanded and developed the business — to become, at turn of century, Canada's foremost publisher of numismatic catalogues and of guides and listings relating to other present-day collectables.

Of course, we all realize, there simply is no way that I can adequately acknowledge all such memories. I do, however, want to express my gratitude to all, individuals and groups, who have contributed and supported me in whatever success I may have attempted or achieved.

Canadian Coin and Stamp World, April 1963
Headlines refer to the Provincial Quebec Numismatic Auction held
at the Sherbrooke Hotel, Sherbrooke, Quebec on May 10th-11th, 1963

The Charlton
Standard Catalogue

# of Canadian
Colonial Tokens

1st Edition $19.95

The Charlton Standard Catalogue of Canadian Colonial Tokens, First Edition (1988)

Appendix A

JAMES EDWARD CHARLTON

A Chronology

Born Toronto, 26 July 1911.

Attended Balmy Beach and Williamson Road Public Schools, Malvern Collegiate and Central Technical School.

Employed, Rous & Mann, Printers, Simcoe Street, Toronto, March 1928 to November 1928.

Employed, Miller Lithographic Company, 100 King Street West, Toronto, December 1928 to August 1929.

Employed, Canadian National Express, Riverdale Station, Toronto, September 1929 to June 1930.

Roselawn Dairy, Gladstone Avenue and Van Horne Street, Toronto, assistant boiler room engineer, December 1930 to August 1933.

International Nickel Company, Ontario [Copper] Refinery, Copper Cliff, Ontario, operating and maintenance engineer, 28 August 1933 to 14 January 1940, residence in Sudbury.

International Nickel Company, Levack Mine, Levack, Ontario, boiler room chief engineer, 15 January 1940 to 20 October 1940, residence in Levack.

Defence Industries Limited, Light, Heat and Power Department, Nobel, Ontario, initially as shift engineer, subsequently as chief engineer in charge of operations, 21 October 1940 to August 1945. Residence in Nobel, except for April to November 1944, when serving as chief engineer at a plant in Brantford, Ontario, producing glycerine for the war effort.

Atomic Energy Plant, Chalk River, Ontario, power house chief engineer, August 1945 to 31 March 1948, residence in Deep River.

Toronto Star, 80 King Street West, Toronto, chief engineer, 2 April 1948 to 1 April 1961, residence in Toronto.

Commercial business, Canada Coin Exchange, inaugurated from Toronto residence, 1949.

Store, office and warehouse, 53 Front Street East, Toronto, 2 August 1956 to 31 October 1958.

Business relocated to 80 Richmond Street East, Toronto, 31 October 1958 to August 1965.

International Coin Company acquired, May 1963.

Retail store and office at 49 Queen Street East, Toronto, opened 26 June 1963. Warehouse remained at Richmond Street location.

Operations at Queen Street store and office and Richmond Street warehouse transferred to 92 Jarvis Street, August 1965.

Charlton Coin and Stamp Supply business sold to J. Alexander Forbes, 2 July 1967.

Arcade Coin Store business operated from February 1963 until sold to Frank Rose in 1968.

Canadian Coin Exchange business sold to Richard Robinson and Fred Samuels, 1 May 1969.

Charlton retirement really began with completion of the 1969 C.N.A. Convention Auction.

Appendix B

JIM CHARLTON AND ORGANIZED NUMISMATICS

Canadian Numismatic Association
Joined, 1950, as member 53.
Life member 6.
Attended 1953 annual meeting and all 47 conventions, 1954 to 2000.
Recipient, J. Douglas Ferguson Award gold medal, 1972.
C.N.A. banquet speaker, educational seminar participant and exhibit judge.
President, 1977 to 1979.

Canadian Paper Money Society
Life member.
Honorary Vice-President.

Ontario Numismatic Association
Member 18.
Recipient, Award of Merit gold medal, 1967.

American Numismatic Association
Life member.
Certified exhibit judge.
50 Year Gold Medal, 2000.
Presidential Award, 2000.

Professional Numismatic Guild of Canada
Honorary member No. 1.

Canadian Association of Numismatic Dealers
Honorary Member.

Canadian Association of Token Collectors
Member

Canadian Association of Wooden Money Collectors
Member

Pre-Retirement Affiliations
Royal Numismatic Society, fellow, from 1960.
Professional Numismatists Guild, member.
International Association of Professional Numismatists, member.
Organzation of International Numismatists, director.
International Bank Note Society, member.

Numismatic Literary Guild
Charter life member.

Royal Canadian Mint
Participant, two coinage design selection committees.
Recipient, Royal Canadian Mint Medal, for numismatic education, 1988.

Business and Publishing Activities

Owner and operator, Canada Coin Exchange, 1949 to 1969; Arcade Coin Store, 1963 to 1968;

and Charlton Coin & Stamp Company Limited.

Numismatic auctioneer, 1954 to 1969; mail auctions, 1950 to 1953.

Editor, *Charlton Standard Catalogue of Canadian Coins*, 1952 to 1980.

Editor, *Canadian and Newfoundland Paper Money*, catalogue, 1954.

Editor, *Charlton Coin Guide*, 1961 to 1980.

Co-editor, *Charlton-Willey Standard Grading Guide to Canadian Decimal Coins*, 1965.

Canadian Editor and "Canadian Trends" editor and columnist, *Coin World*, 1961 to 1969,

and subsequently.

Coin columnist for major Toronto newspapers, *Toronto Star* and *The Telegram.*

Service as Numismatic Expert Witness

Supreme Court of Nova Scotia. *Le Chameau* Treasure Case, 1973

Tax Court of Canada, Calgary. Appeal of Revenue Canada valuation of numismatic donation, 1987.

Appendix C

Jim Charlton's First 47 National Canadian Conventions

Canadian Numismatic Association, 1954-2000

1954	Toronto	1978	London
1955	Ottawa	1979	Edmonton
1956	London	1980	Montreal
1957	Hamilton	1981	Toronto
1958	Ottawa	1982	Winnipeg
1959	Regina	1983	Moncton
1960	Sherbrooke	1984	Hamilton
1961	Hamilton	1985	Regina
1962	Detroit	1986	Toronto
1963	Vancouver	1987	Calgary
1964	Halifax	1988	Charlottetown
1965	Montreal	1989	Quebec City
1966	Winnipeg	1990	Vancouver
1967	Ottawa	1991	Toronto
1968	Calgary	1992	Montreal
1969	Toronto	1993	Moncton
1970	Halifax	1994	Hamilton
1971	Vancouver	1995	Calgary
1972	Toronto	1996	Montreal
1973	Saskatoon	1997	Moncton
1974	Hamilton	1998	Edmonton
1975	Calgary	1999	Kitchener
1976	Ottawa	2000	Ottawa
1977	Vancouver		

Appendix D

Some Relevant Canadian Readings

The Coins and Tokens of Canada, Wayte Raymond, three editions, 1937, 1947, 1952.

Canadian Numismatic Coin Topics, Bert Koper, 1938 and subsequent releases.

Canadian Provicinal Cents, 1858-1859, Bert Koper.

1942 Tombac Nickels, Bert Koper.

Canadian Tokens and Medals, A. D. Hoch, from *The Numismatist*, new writings on Canadian numismatics.

McCready's Paper Money Record, A. L. McCready, issues of June, September, 1949.

Canadian Banks and Bank Notes, C. S. Howard.

Canadian Coin Catalogue, Neil Carmichael, 1953.

Canadian and Newfoundland Currency, 1866-1954, J. A. Elliot, Jr., 1955. Subsequent illustrated release, 1955.

Medals Awarded to North American Indian Chiefs, 1714-1922. Jamieson.

A Guide Book of Canadian Coins, Currency & Tokens, Somer James and H. C. Taylor, 1959.

Canadian Patterns, Fred Bowman, 1957.

Canadian Numismatic Digest, Montreal Coin Club, for National Coin Week, 1960.

Wooden Money of Canada, Larry Gingras, 1961. Supplement, 1963.

Canadian Silver Dollars, Starr Gilmore, edited by H. C. Taylor and Somer James, 1961.

The Ships, Colonies & Commerce Tokens of Canada, a revision of W. A. Lee's classification, published by Walter G. Holmes in collaboration with Sheldon Carroll and Lorne R. Wilson, 1963.

A Guide for the Grading of Canadian Coins, Cecil S. Paul and Gerald B. Parker, 1964.

Communion Tokens of the Presbyterian Church in Canada, Fred Bowman, 1965.

The Simplified Grading Guide for the Coins of Canada and Newfoundland, Hans Zoell, assisted by Cec Tannahill and Barry Benwick, 1965.

My 2 Cents Worth, Jack Veffer.

Treasury Notes of the Colony of British Columbia, Willard E. Ireland and Ronald A. Greene, 1966.

The Tokens of British Columbia and the Yukon, Vancouver Numismatic Society, 1969.

War Medals and Decorations of Canada, Ross W. Irwin, 1969.

Coins of Canada, J. A. Haxby and R. C. Willey, from 1971. Yearly editions.

Trade Tokens of Ontario, Fred Bowman, 1972.

Tokens of Quebec, Fred Bowman, 1972.

The Decimal Coinage of Nova Scotia, New Brunswick and Prince Edward Island, J. Richard Becker, 1975.

Medals, Tokens and Paper Money of the Hudson's Bay Company, Larry Gingras, 1975.

Medals and Tokens of Industrial Exhibition of Toronto, Norman E. Wells, 1975.

The Prince Edward Island Tree Cent, Earle K. Kennedy, 1976.

Franco-American Jetons, Ed. Frossard, reprinted 1977, by Katen; reprinted also by Maurice Lorrain.

Silver and Nickel Dollars of Canada, 1911 to Date, Stephan E. Dushnik, 1978.

Medals, Dora de Pedery-Hunt.

The 1980 Charlton Canadian Trade Dollar Guide, Serge Pelletier, 1st edition, 1980. Released as *Standard Catalogue of Canadian Municipal Trade Tokens and Notes*, 3rd edition, 1993.

Striking Impressions: The Royal Canadian Mint and Canadian Coinage, James A. Haxby, 1984.

La Monnaie Canadienne, Yvon Marquis, 1985.

Aspects of the Numismatics of North America, C. F. Gilboy and the Regina Coin Club, 1986.

Alberta Trade Tokens, Donald M. Stewart, 1987.

Canadian Numismatics, quarterly periodical, March 1988 through Fall 1989.

Canadian Trade Dollars, Jean-Guy Côté, 1991, 1994, 1995.

Canadian Coins and Paper Money, Will Gandley, 8th edition, 1996.

Dictionary of Canadian Medallists, Robert C. Willey, edited by Ronald Greene, 1998.

Appendix E

Canadian Stamps, Coins, Tokens, Paper Money

Price List No. 3

1938

Sheldon S. Carroll
Norwich, Ontario, Canada

Member of
Stamp Collectors' Exchange Club
Winnipeg Numismatic Art Society

CANADIAN COINS

My stock of Canadian Coins is changing all the time. Coins are going out and more are coming in every week. If you don't see what you want, send me your want list, and I'll help you. These coins are numbered according to Breton.

Jetons

Breton No.	Fair	Good	Fine	Unc.
510 Louis XV and Indian among lilies; copper			3.50	

Quebec

Breton No.	Fair	Good	Fine	Unc
520 Magdalen Island Token	.50		2.00	
521 Penny Token, Province du Bas Canada, 1837				
City Bank	.07	.13		
Bank of Montreal	.07			
Quebec Bank	.07	.13		
522 Half Penny Token, Province du Bas				
Canada, 1837	.05	.10	.20	
City Bank	.05	.10	.20	
Bank of Montreal	.05	.10		
Quebec Bank	.05	.10		
526 Penny Token, Bank of Montreal, 1842	.20	.40		
527 Half Penny Token, Bank of Montreal				
1842	.04	.08	.15	
1844	.04	.08	.15	
528 Penny Token, Quebec Bank, 1852	.07	.13	.25	
529 Half Penny Token, Quebec Bank, 1852		.08	.15	

Bouquet Sous

Breton No.		Fair	Good	Fine	Unc
678	Agriculture and Commerce, Wreath of 16 leaves		.65		
679	Agriculture and Commerce, Wreath of 16 leaves	.35			
684	Agriculture and Commerce, Wreath of 17 leaves			.65	
686	Agriculture and Commerce, Wreath of 18 leaves	.35			
688	Agriculture and Commerce, Wreath of 18 leaves			.45	
691	Agriculture and Commerce, Wreath of 18 leaves	.25		1.00	
692	Agriculture and Commerce, Wreath of 18 leaves	.25	.50		
693	Agriculture and Commerce, Wreath of 18 leaves	.25			
694	Agriculture and Commerce, Wreath of 18 leaves		.50		
704	Agriculture and Commerce, Wreath of 20 leaves		.45		
713	Trade and Agriculture	.07			
714	Trade and Agriculture	.07			
715	Agriculture and Commerce, Banque de Peuple	.07	.13	.25	

Ontario

Breton No.		Fair	Good	Fine	Unc
719	Penny Token, Bank of Upper Canada				
	1850	.04	.08	.15	
	1852	.04	.08	.15	
	1854	.04	.07	.15	
	1857	.04	.08	.15	
720	Half Penny Token, Bank of Upper Canada				
	1850		.05	.10	
	1852	.03	.05	.10	
	1854		.05	.10	
	1857		.05	.10	.20
721	Brock Token — Ship and Inscription		.13		
727	Half Penny Token, Ship, Anvil, Tools, 1820		.13		
730	Half Penny Token, Plow, 1833	.07	.13		

Province of Canada

Breton No.		Fair	Good	Fine	Unc
866	Queen Victoria, 1 Cent, 1859	.04	.08	.15	

Nova Scotia

Breton No.		Fair	Good	Fine	Unc
867	Half Penny Token, 1823	.07			
868	Penny Token, 1824	.07			
870	Penny Token, 1832	.07	.13		
871	Half Penny Token, 1832	.04	.08	.15	
873	Penny Token, Victoria, 1840		.13		
874	Half Penny Token, Victoria, 1849		.08	.15	
875	Penny Token, 1856		.13		
876	Half Penny Token, 1856	.04	.08	.15	
878	Half Cent				
	1861		.13	.25	
	1864		.13	.25	
883	Half Penny Token, Hosterman and Etter, 1815	.07	.13		
884	Half Penny Token, Starr and Shannon, 1815			.25	
886	Half Penny Token, Genuine British Copper, 1815	.10			

New Brunswick

Breton No.		Fair	Good	Fine	Unc
909	Penny Token, 1843		.13		
910	Half Penny Token, 1843		.13		

Prince Edward Island

		Fair	Good	Fine	Unc
915	One Cent, 1871			.15	
917	Success to the Fisheries, Speed the Plow	.04	.08	.15	
918	Prince Edward Island, 1855		.08		
919	Prince Edward Island, 1857	.04			
920	One Cent, Fisheries and Agriculture, 1855			.15	

Dominion of Canada

Breton No.		Fair	Good	Fine	Unc
943	5 Cents, silver, Victoria	.08			
	1874	.08			
	1893	.08			
	1900	.08			
	1901		.12	.15	
944	1 Cent, copper, Victoria. I have all the dates from 1876-1901.	.03	.05	.10	

Newfoundland

Breton No.		Fair	Good	Fine	Unc
951	1 Cent, Victoria				.10

Miscellaneous

Breton No.		Fair	Good	Fine	Unc
960	Half penny token, 1812	.07	.13		
961	Token with no inscription, 1812	.07			
965	Half Penny — Trade and Navigation, 1813		.13		
967	Copper Preferable to Paper, 1838	.07			
979	Half Penny, Wellington	.07			
981	Half Penny, Illustrious Wellington, 1816	.15			
987	Wellington (list of battles on reverse)		.13	.25	
994	Half Penny Token, Eagle, 1815	.07	.13		
997	Ships, Colonies and Commerce	.07	.13	.25	.50
1012	Harp Token, 1820		.13		
1013	North America Token, 1781	.13			

Canadian Silver Dollars (Uncirculated)

Breton No.	Fair	Good	Fine	Unc
1935 Jubilee				2.00
1936				2.00
1937				2.00

Paper Money

Breton No.	Fair	Good	Fine	Unc
Zimmerman Bank, Clifton, $3.00, 1850				
(good condition)				.45
Dominion of Canada, 25¢, 1900 or 1923				
(good condition)				.50

Appendix F

CANADA COIN EXCHANGE
Box 35, Terminal "A"
Toronto, Canada

PRICE LIST
Prices good until 31 December 1949
or present stock

Guarantee: All coins are guaranteed genuine. All coins not entirely satisfactory returnable within five days after receipt. Our 100% guarantee protects you.

Quotations: All want lists given close attention. Prices quoted are good as long as stock lasts or can be replenished. If you do not see coins listed that you need, please write. Every effort will be made to supply your needs.

Terms: Send payment with order. Money orders preferred; or, if currency, registered mail. Postage 15¢ extra on orders under $2.00. All orders appreciated, no matter how small.

Note: Due to the premium on American money, we allow a 10% discount on all purchases paid in U.S. funds, less 15¢ bank charge on cheques. Please add supplementary list in case some of the coins you are not in stock. We have a large variety of American, English and foreign coins, and will be glad to send list or lists upon request. We will answer questions on coins free of charge. Please enclose 4¢ stamp with enquiries.

CONDITIONS OF COINS

B.U. (Brilliant Uncirculated) — A coin in brilliant new condition, never in circulation.

UNC. (Uncirculated) — A coin never in circulation, but not brilliant.

V.F. (Very Fine) — A coin from circulation, but only slightest or no signs of wear.

F. (Fine) — Showing slightest sign of wear, all lettering clear.

V.G. (Very Good) — Somewhat worn but still desirable, all lettering readable.

G. (Good) — Considerably worn, all type readable, except for 5 cent and 10 cent silver.

FAIR — Badly worn, and type does not all show.

POOR — Coins that have become very badly worn, damaged, bent, scratched, holed, or nicked. Can be used as space fillers. Dates clear on some.

CANADIAN COINS, CURRENCY AND TOKENS

1949 Uncirculated Coin Set: $1.00, 50¢, 25¢, 10¢, 5¢, 1¢. $2.90

Large size $1 notes: 1923 – $1.50 for Good, $1.75 for Crisp Unc.
  1917 – $1.75 for Very Good.

Large size $2 notes: 1923 – $2.50 for Good, $2.75 for Crisp Unc.

25¢ notes: 1870 – $1.50 for good. **1900** – 60¢ for Good. **1923** –
50¢ for Good, 75¢ for Fine.

Silver Dollars, VG to Unc. 1935, $1.50. 1936, $1.50. 1937, $1.50,
1938, $2.00, 1939, $1.50. 1945, $2.00. 1946, $1.50. 1947,
$1.75. 1948, $2.50. 1949, $1.40. Set of ten, $17.00

Complete set of large nickels, 1922-1949, 30 coins, F to Unc.
$3.50. 25 different, $2.25, Wartime tombac nickels, 1942 & 43,
F, 10¢ each, Br.Unc., 25¢ each.

Complete set of large & small cents. 1858-1949, 72 coins, VG to
Unc., $8.00.

Complete set of Large Cents, 1858-1920, 42 coins, VG to VF, $5.00

Set of Large Cents, 1858 to 1901, 22 coins, $4.00. 10 different, VG
to F, $1.50.

Set of Large Cents, 1902-1920, coins, VG to F, $1.00, or 5¢ each.

Large Cents, 30 different, includes former 20, plus 10 from 1859 to
1901, $2.25.

Small Cents, set, 1920-1949, 30 coins, G to Unc, $3.00. 20
different, $1.00. 25 different, $1.50.

Five Cents, Silver, 1902-1920, average VG, 10 different. $1.00. 10¢
each. 15 different, 1902-1920, includes 1902 and 1911, $2.00,
1902 Queen's Crown Error, 20 ¢. 1911, without "Dei Gra," 20 ¢.
Our selection, 20¢ each, 5 different, average VG, $1.00.

Complete set of Upper Canada Tokens, 1850-1857, 8 pieces, F,
$2.00. Includes ½ penny, 1 penny, 1850, 1852, 1854, 1857.
1 penny, VG - F, 30¢. ½ penny, VG - F, 20¢.

Early Canadian Tokens, Wellington, Brock, etc, 1812 to 1844,
average VG. 5 different, $1.00. 12 different, $2.50. 20 different,
$4.00.

Early Canadian Sous. 1837, Deux Sous or 1 penny, VG, 35¢; G,
25¢. Un Sous or ½ penny, 1837, and others Minted without
dates, F, 35¢; VG, 25¢; G, 20¢; Fair, 15¢.

Nova Scotia. 1 penny, VG, 30¢; Fair, 20¢; ½ penny, VG, 25¢; G,
20¢. Fair, 15¢. Cents, VG to F, 20¢; G, 15¢; Fair, 10¢.

New Brunswick. ½ penny, F, 30¢; Fair, 15¢. Cent, VG, 20¢.

Prince Edward Island. ½ penny, VG, 25¢; G, 20¢; Fair, 15¢.

Canada, 25 cents, silver. Before 1902, date(s) of our selection, F,
$1.00; VG, 75¢, 1902 and later, date(s) of our selection, F, 60¢;
VG, 40¢.

Special Set of 20 cents, silver. Canada, 1858; New Brunswick,
1862 and 1864; Newfoundland, 1896. Average VG, $5.00.

Newfoundland. Large cents. Before 1904 15¢. 1904 and later, VG to
F, 10¢. Five cents, silver. Before 1912, 20¢. 1912 and later, G to
VF, 15¢. Twenty cents, silver. Before 1912, 60¢. 1912 G to F,
50¢. Fifty cents, silver, date(s) of our selection, VG to F, 75¢.

Appendix G

CANADA COIN EXCHANGE
Box 35, Terminal "A"
Toronto, Ontario

JUNE 1951 PRICE LIST
[Selected Offerings]

All material offered subject to prior sale and to change in price after June 30th.

All material guaranteed satisfactory or money refunded, if claim is made within five days after receipt.

Please allow 20¢ for registration on orders under $5.00.

CANADIAN PAPER MONEY
Government Issues

Dominion of Canada, $1, 1870, Jacques Cartier, VG, $7.00.
Dominion of Canada, $1, 1878, Countess of Dufferin, VG-F, $5.
Dominion of Canada, $1, 1898, Earl & Countess of Aberdeen, VG, $3.50.
Dominion of Canada, $1, 1911, Earl & Countess Grey, VG, $2.50
Dominion of Canada, $1, 1917, Princess Patricia, Ab F, $3.00.
    Similar, black seal, VG, $2.25.
Dominion of Canada, $1, 1923, McCavour-Saunders, red seal, Unc, $4.00. Seven other varieties listed.
Dominion of Canada, $2, 1878, Earl of Dufferin, Fair, corner off, and portion at top $5.50
Dominion of Canada, $2, 1887, Marquess & Marchioness of Lansdowne, VG, but mended, $5.50.
Dominion of Canada, $2, 1897, Edward, Prince of Wales, later King Edward VII, VG, $3.25.
Dominion of Canada, $2, 1914, Duke & Duchess Connaught, F, $3.50. Similar, black seal, VG-F, $3.50.
Dominion of Canada, $2, 1923, Campbell-Sellar, black seal, Unc, $4.00. Seven other varieties listed.
Dominion of Canada, $4, 1904, Ship in locks, VG, $9.50.
Dominion of Canada, $5, 1912, Train, VG, $6.50.
Dominion of Canada, $5, 1924, Queen Mary, VF, $7.25.
Dominion of Canada, $500, 1925, King George V, F-VF, $515.00.
Government of Newfoundland, $1, 1920, King George V, VG, $3.75.

Chartered Bank Note Issues, Negotiable

Canadian Bank of Commerce, $5, 1917, Unc, $7.25.
Banque Canadienne Nationale, $20, 1929, VG-F, $22.00.
Dominion Bank, $5, 1938, XF, $6.00.
Imperial Bank of Canada, 1939, $5, VG, $5.25.
Bank of Montreal, $10, 1923, VG-F, $11.25.

Bank of Nova Scotia, $5, 1918, VF, but trimmed close at bottom, $6.25.
Provincial Bank of Canada, $5, 1936, F-VF, $5.75.
Quebec Bank, $1, 1863, G, $3.75.
Royal Bank of Canada, $10, 1927, Ab Unc, $12.25.
Standard Bank, $5, 1919, VG, $6.00.
Bank of Toronto, $10, 1937, Ab Unc, $11.00
Traders Bank, $5, 1897, F, $7.50
Union Bank, Winnipeg, $5, 1897, F, $7.50.

Note Issues, Nonredeemable

Bank of Acadia, Liverpool, $4, G, but upper right corner missing, $4.00.
Agricultural Bank, Toronto, $5, 1835, F-VF, $3.50.
Bank of Brantford, $5, 1859, VG, $4.00.
Bank of Clifton, $2, 1861, Unc, $3.50.
City Bank, Montreal, $10, 1856, VG, $9.00.
Colonial Bank, Toronto, $5, 1859, Unc, $4.00.
Consolidated Bank, Montreal, $10, 1876, Fair, $7.00.
Cuvillier & Sons, Montreal, $1, unsigned, Unc, $4.50.
Distillerie de St. Denis, Montreal, 60 sous, 1837, VG, $2.50.
Exchange Bank of Toronto, $5, 1855, unsigned, VG-F, $4.75.
Farmers Bank of Rustico, $1, 1872, VG, $5.00.
Farmers Joint Stock Bank, Toronto, $5, 1849, F-VF, $3.50.
Henry's Bank, Montreal, $1, 1837, VF, $4.25.
Kingston Bank, $5, F-VF, $3.50.
Macdonald & Co., Victoria, $5, 1863, VG, $11.00.
Bank of Prince Edward Island, Charlottetown, $10, 1872, VG, $8.00.
Union Bank, Montreal, $2, Ab VG, $3.00.
Bank of Upper Canada, Toronto, $1, Unc, small portion of corner and edge off, $2.50.
Bank of Western Canada, Clifton, $1, 1859, VG-F, $4.00.
Westmorland Bank, Moncton, $1, 1861, Unc, signature crossed out, $6.75.
Zimmerman Bank, Elgin, $5, Fair, $3.00.

Gold

Canada, $5, 1912, Ab Unc, minute file marks, $14.50.
Canada, $5, 1913, Ab Unc, minute file marks, $15.00.
Canada, $5, 1913, Ab Unc, minute file marks, $16.50.
Canada, $10, 1912, Ab Unc, minute file marks, $29.50.
Newfoundland, $2, 1870, VF-XF, $12.25.
Newfoundland, $2, 1872, XF, $13.50.
England, Spade Guinea, 1788, VG-F, but holed, $11.50.
England, Sovereign, 1908, Ab Unc, $12.50.
United States, $10, 1911, Ab Unc, minute file marks, $26.00.

Miscellaneous

Breton Catalogue, 1912, paper cover, like new, $7.50.

Early Canadian tokens, damaged or badly worn, 100 mixed, $5.00.

Condor and Provincial Tokens of England, average F, 10 different, $2.00. Same in VG, 10 different, $1.50.

United States Civil War Cents and Tradesmen's Tokens, F-VF, 10 different, $2.00.

Foreign Coins, 10 different silver crowns, F-VF, $14.50.

Canada, 1914-18 Bronze Star, issued to lieutenant, $3.50.

Canada, 1939-45 Defence Medal, silver, $1.50.

Canada, 1939-45, Victory Medal, silver, $1.50.

Newfoundland, 50¢ pieces, average VG-F, mixed, 20 for $13.00.

Appendix H

Canadian Numismatic Association 1954
Convention
Auction Highlights
Prices Realised

Canada

Large Cents

1858, Unc	$13.00
1907H, Unc	8.50

Small Cent

1922, Unc	5.25

5 Cents

1871, Unc	8.00

10 Cents

1871H, Unc	10.25
1902H, Unc	3.50
1936, Unc	3.60

20 Cents

1858, Unc	9.50

25 Cents

1870, Unc	7.25
1902H, Unc	6.25

50 Cents

1872, Unc	15.50

Silver Dollars

1938, Unc	8.50
1945, Unc	8.50
1945, Br Proof	18.50
1947, ML, Unc	9.00
1947, Pt 7, Unc	12.00
1948, Br Proof	17.00

Gold

$5, 1914, Unc	29.00
$10, 1914, Unc	42.25
Set, $5 and $10, 1912, 1913, 1914, Unc	$215.00
Sovereign, 1911C, Unc	80.00

Specimen Set, 1¢ to $1

1937, Cased	32.50

Canadian Paper Money

Province of Canada

$1, 1866, Fine, but tiny hole	$25.00

Dominion of Canada

$1, 1911, Unc	$10.75
$1, 1923, lilac sel, AU	$12.00
$2, 1878, F/VG	$18.00
$2, 1887, VG-F	$12.00
$2, 1914, Saunders, VF	$11.00
$4, 1900, VG, but sl. nick	$25.00
$5, 1912, Boville, Unc	$16.50

Newfoundland
    40 cents, 1907, VG, but sl. nick $18.50
    Bank of Canada
    English, $1, Unc $5.00
    English, $2, Unc. $7.75
    English, $20, AU $23.50
    Bank of Montreal, $1, 1849, XF $51.00
    Bank of New Brunswick, $5, 1904, abt F $23.00
    Bank of New Brunswick, $10, 1903, abt. F $31.00
    Quebec Bank, $1, 1860 F-VF $30.00
    Standard Bank, $20, 1919, VF $30.00
    Union Bank of Lower Canada, $, 1866, F $26.00
    Union Bank, $10, 1893 $40.00
    Bank of Brantford, Sault Ste. Marie,
        $1, 2, 4, 5, 1859, Unc $20.00
Bank of Upper Canada, $1, 1854, VG-F $16.25
Hudson's Bay Co., 5 shillings, Unc $14.40

Appendix I

Membership in the CANTEL Canadian Teletype Circuit

Van Horne Sales Ltd.
Place Ville Marie
Montreal, Quebec
Mr. Fred Samuels

Imperial Coin
Salem, New Hampshire
Mr. D. Green

Numismatic Investments of Canada
Ltd.
Montreal, Quebec
Mr. P. Lazanik

Walter C. Edwards Coin Shop Inc.
Parma, Ohio
Mr. W. C. Edwards

La Cie des Numismates Laval Inc.
Montreal 18, Quebec
Mr. Michael Todascu

Baily Coins
Montreal, Quebec
Mr. Larry Baily

The Money Shop
University Heights 18, Ohio
Mr. Louis M. Irwin

Goldsmith Rare Coin Shop
Montreal, Quebec
Mr. Louis Goldsmith

Universal Coin
Toronto, Ontario
Mr. John Kone

Canada Coin Exchange
Toronto, Ontario
Mr. J. E. Charlton

Colony Coins
Cleveland, Ohio
Mr. Don Billar

Kathleen W. Dowd
Saratoga Springs, New York

C. F. Martin
Sudbury, Ontario

Ryan Coin Shop
Chicago, Illinois
Mr. T. Ryan

M & M Coin (International) Co.
Toronto 1, Ontario
Mrs. Margot Mushell

Spiers' Coin Dealers
Mr. Phil Spier

Meyrand Investments Corp.
Pittsburgh 35, Pennsylvania
Mr. A. Godispot

Rockland Coin Co. (Regd)
Montreal 16, Quebec
Mr. M. de Abravanel

Red Cent Coin Company
Toronto, Ontario
Mr. William K. Cross

John T. Abbott
Detroit 20, Michigan

Jay M. Weisman
Scranton, Pennsylvania

Pashkow, Beer & Company
Philadelphia, Pennsylvania
Mr. F. Pashkow

Holloway House
Eastview, Ontario
Mr. F. Holloway

Lloyds International Coin Exchange
Lord Simcoe Hotel
Toronto 1, Ontario
Mr. M. Mitchell

Provincial Coin Co. Ltd.
Hamilton, Ontario
Mr. Roy Lehman

Coinatorium
Montreal, Quebec
Mr. L. Lazanik

Border Coin Company
Newport, Vermont
Mr. G. Gosselin

National Capital Coin Co. Ltd.
Ottawa, Ontario
Mr. G. Knapp

Danny's Coins and Stamps
Hamilton, Ontario
Mr. D. Hrincu

Loga Ltd.
Niagara Falls, Ontario
Mr. J. F. Newton

Castle Coin Co. Reg'd
Montreal 26, Quebec
Mr. L. Sacharen

National Coin Exchange Reg'd
Montreal, Quebec
Mr. E. Bernstein

Ottawa Coins
Ottawa, Ontario
Mr. Peter DeGraaf

Collectors Centre
Toronto 2, Ontario
Mr. A. Rosen

Maple Leaf Collectors Exchange Ltd.
Montreal, Quebec
Mr. R. Hello

H Lipson & Sons Reg'd
C.N.R. Station
Montreal, Quebec
Mr. H. Lipson

Canada Proof Like Sets
Toronto, Ontario
Mr. A. Robins

Ernie Lush
Union Lake, Michigan

Ray Hobin
Stittsville, Ontario

A. Rex Coins
Toronto, Ontario
Mr. B. Resimich

Kay's Coins
Windsor, Ontario
Mr. M. Scott

Mark's Rare Coins Reg'd
Quebec, Quebec
Mr. Marl Thivierge

```
CC   HERE  NOW  CC   OUT
CA   TO    CC   CC   CC
JIM  CONGRATULATIONS    ON   A   JOB   WELL
DONE ON  UR   AUCTION   NEVER  SAW   ANY   THING
D  SO   NICE     THX  FOR  THE   CAD  LEW  AT   CA   OUT
```

Relic of the teletype era? Congratulations from dealer
Lew Goldsmith on the C.N.A. 1965 Auction outcome

Appendix J

CKFH RADIO
5000 W, 1430 kHz
TORONTO

Program:	Keys to Safety
Time:	Mondays A.M., 10 to 11
Client:	Canada Coin Exchange
Date:	October 7 to November 4, 1963

RADIO CONTINUITY

FUN AND PROFIT - THAT'S AN UNBEATABLE COMBINATION — AND IF YOU'VE DISCOVERED THE DELIGHTFUL HOBBY OF COIN COLLECTING - YOU'LL KNOW THIS IS THE CATEGORY IT FITS INTO. FOR THOSE OF YOU WHO HAVE AS YET TO MAKE THIS DISCOVERY, CONSIDER THE HANDFUL OF COINS IN YOUR POCKET OR PURSE. DO YOU KNOW THE REAL VALUE OF THESE COINS? WOULD YOU RECOGNIZE A VALUABLE COIN IF YOU RECEIVED ONE, OR WOULD YOU SPEND IT, COMPLETELY UNAWARE OF THE VALUE? BEGIN COIN COLLECTING AS A HOBBY TODAY. YOU'LL BE COLLECTING MONEY, AND WHAT COULD BE MORE ENJOYABLE. IT REALLY IS A FASCINATING AND PROFITABLE HOBBY, AND THE FIRST STEP IN BEGINNING IT YOURSELF, IS TO PAY A VISIT TO CANADA COIN EXCHANGE, 40 QUEEN STREET EAST, WHERE YOU'LL FIND THE WORLD'S MOST COMPLETE LINE OF NUMISMATIC BOKS AND ACCESSORIES. MAKE THIS THE DAY YOU START A HOBBY THAT WILL PAY. VISIT THE CANADA COIN EXCHANGE AT 49 QUEEN STREET EAST, OR SEND 50 CENTS FOR YOUR COPY OF THE 1964 COIN GUIDE.

Revision October 14

Appendix K

Jim Charlton's Auctions

I.

Mail Bid Auction Sales of Canada Coin Exchange

No. 1.   22 May 1950
No. 2   30 September 1950
No. 3   30 November 1950
No. 4   31 March 1951
No. 5   29 September 1951
No. 6   29 March 1952
No. 7   24 November 1952
No. 8   21 November 1953

II.

C.N.A. Convention Auction Sales

1954	Toronto	23-24 August
1955	Ottawa	5-6 September
1956	London	21-22 September
1957	Hamilton	30-31 August
1958	Ottawa	4-6 September
1959	Regina	2-4 September
1960	Sherbrooke	18-20 August
1961	Hamilton	31 August - 2 September
1962	Detroit	15-18 August
1964	Halifax	27-29 August
1965	Montreal	12-14 August
1966	Winnipeg	25-27 August
1967	Ottawa	31 August - 2 September
1968	Calgary	15-17 July
1969	Toronto	28-30 August

III.

Canada Coin Exchange Auctions

1962   Province of Quebec Numismatic Association founding convention, Montreal, 25-26 May.

1962   Greater Toronto Coin and Stamp Exhibition, Toronto, 23-24 November.

1963   Province of Quebec Numismatic Association convention, Sherbrooke, 10-11 May.

1963   Toronto Coin Club Fall Rally, Toronto, 23 November.

1964   Empire State Numismatic Association convention, Buffalo, 22-24 May.

1964   Toronto Coin Club Fall Rally, Toronto, 17 October.

1966   Central Coin Club, Toronto, 22-23 April.

1966   Central Coin Club, Toronto, 8 October

1968   Nickel Belt Coin Club and Sudbury Stamp Society, Sudbury, 13 April.

APPENDIX L

50-YEAR PRICE RANGE OF 16 SELECTED CANADIAN COINS

	Large Cent 1858		Large Cent 1891 Large Leaves Small Date		Small Cent 1923	
	VG	Unc	VG	Unc	VG	Unc
1952 (1st)	0.75	3.00	2.25	7.00	1.00	4.50
1953 (2nd)	1.25	6.00	6.00	30.00	1.25	5.00
1955 (3rd)	2.50	9.00	9.00	50.00	1.25	8.00
1956 (4th)	2.50	11.00	11.00	55.00	2.25	10.00
1957 (5th)	2.50	12.00	12.00	60.00	2.25	15.00
1958 (6th)	5.00	15.00	17.00	70.00	2.00	20.00
1959 (7th)	8.00	20.00	20.00	80.00	2.00	25.00
1960 (8th)	9.00	25.00	25.00	115.00	2.50	50.00
1961 (9th)	10.00	30.00	25.00	150.00	3.00	60.00
1962 (10th)	10.00	35.00	25.00	150.00	4.50	75.00
1963 (11th)	14.00	40.00	30.00	175.00	15.00	85.00
1964 (12th)	20.00	40.00	30.00	175.00	15.00	85.00
1965 (13th)	25.00	80.00	30.00	225.00	15.00	125.00
1966 (14th)	25.00	90.00	30.00	225.00	14.00	125.00
1967 (15th)	25.00	90.00	30.00	225.00	11.00	125.00
1968 (16th)	23.00	85.00	30.00	200.00	10.00	115.00
1969 (17th)	23.00	85.00	30.00	200.00	10.00	115.00
1970 (18th)	20.00	85.00	30.00	200.00	10.00	115.00
1971 (19th)	20.00	85.00	30.00	200.00	10.00	115.00
1972 (20th)	18.00	165.00	28.00	200.00	8.50	115.00
1973 (21st)	16.00	80.00	25.00	175.00	8.50	115.00
1974 (22nd)	15.00	75.00	25.00	160.00	9.50	115.00
1975 (23rd)	15.00	75.00	25.00	160.00	10.00	115.00
1976 (24th)	18.00	90.00	25.00	160.00	15.00	115.00
1977 (25th)	20.00	100.00	25.00	160.00	13.00	125.00
1979 (27th)	22.00	125.00	35.00	200.00	18.00	150.00
1980 (29th)	30.00	150.00	40.00	200.00	18.00	175.00
1981 (31st)	35.00	200.00	45.00	350.00	25.00	225.00
1982 (33rd)	40.00	250.00	45.00	350.00	25.00	225.00
1983 (35tht)	40.00	250.00	50.00	400.00	25.00	250.00
1984 (37th)	40.00	250.00	55.00	400.00	20.00	250.00
1985 (39th)	38.00	200.00	55.00	350.00	20.00	200.00
1987 (41st)	40.00	225.00	65.00	450.00	20.00	225.00
1989 (43rd)	40.00	225.00	65.00	450.00	20.00	225.00
1991 (45th)	40.00	225.00	60.00	450.00	20.00	250.00
1993 (47th)	50.00	300.00	65.00	450.00	22.00	350.00
1995 (49th)	60.00	350.00	80.00	450.00	25.00	300.00
1997 (51st)	60.00	400.00	80.00	550.00	25.00	350.00
1999 (53rd)	60.00	375.00	80.00	550.00	25.00	325.00
2002 (56th)	75.00	450.00	100.00	650.00	30.00	425.00

50-YEAR PRICE RANGE OF 16 SELECTED CANADIAN COINS (cont.)

	5 Cents 1858 Large Date		5 Cents 1921 Silver		5 Cents 1925	
	VG	Unc	VG	Unc	VG	Unc
1952 (1st)	1.25	5.00	45.00	90.00	1.50	7.00
1953 (2nd)	3.00	12.00	45.00	100.00	1.50	10.00
1955 (3rd)	15.00	35.00	50.00	125.00	2.00	12.00
1956 (4th)	18.00	50.00	75.00	175.00	2.50	20.00
1957 (5th)	25.00	60.00	75.00	225.00	2.25	30.00
1958 (6th)	30.00	100.00	125.00	300.00	2.50	50.00
1959 (7th)	40.00	150.00	150.00	400.00	3.00	60.00
1960 (8th)	80.00	200.00	200.00	700.00	4.50	70.00
1961 (9th)	100.00	225.00	250.00	1,000.00	7.00	110.00
1962 (10th)	100.00	225.00	300.00	1,100.00	9.00	125.00
1963 (11th)	100.00	275.00	450.00	2,000.00	19.00	250.00
1964 (12th)	100.00	375.00	600.00	3,000.00	19.00	300.00
1965 (13th)	110.00	375.00	600.00	4,000.00	25.00	375.00
1966 (14th)	110.00	375.00	600.00	4,000.00	23.00	400.00
1967 (15th)	100.00	350.00	600.00	3,000.00	20.00	400.00
1968 (16th)	85.00	315.00	500.00	2,500.00	20.00	350.00
1969 (17th)	100.00	315.00	500.00	2,500.00	20.00	350.00
1970 (18th)	85.00	315.00	500.00	2,500.00	20.00	350.00
1971 (19th)	85.00	315.00	500.00	2,500.00	19.00	350.00
1972 (20th)	80.00	300.00	450.00	2,300.00	16.00	350.00
1973 (21st)	75.00	300.00	400.00	2,300.00	16.00	300.00
1974 (22nd)	80.00	350.00	350.00	2,300.00	16.00	300.00
1975 (23rd)	85.00	350.00	450.00	2,500.00	18.00	300.00
1976 (24th)	85.00	350.00	500.00	3,000.00	20.00	300.00
1977 (25th)	85.00	400.00	1,000.00	4,000.00	22.00	400.00
1979 (27th)	85.00	550.00	1,000.00	4,000.00	25.00	425.00
1980 (29th)	110.00	650.00	1,250.00	6,500.00	30.00	500.00
1981 (31st)	125.00	1,500.00	2,000.00	15,000.00	40.00	900.00
1982 (33rd)	125.00	1,500.00	2,000.00	20,000.00	40.00	900.00
1983 (35th)	125.00	1,500.00	2,000.00	20,000.00	40.00	900.00
1984 (37th)	125.00	1,250.00	2,000.00	20,000.00	35.00	900.00
1985 (39th)	125.00	1,250.00	2,000.00	20,000.00	35.00	800.00
1987 (41st)	150.00	1,350.00	2,000.00	21,000.00	35.00	1,350.00
1989 (43rd)	150.00	1,350.00	2,000.00	20,000.00	35.00	1,400.00
1991 (45th)	135.00	1,200.00	2,000.00	18,000.00	35.00	1,200.00
1993 (47th)	150.00	1,300.00	1,900.00	12,500.00	35.00	1,200.00
1995 (49th)	165.00	2,000.00	2,250.00	12,500.00	35.00	1,250.00
1997 (51st)	175.00	2,250.00	2,250.00	12,500.00	30.00	1,500.00
1999 (53rd)	175.00	1,750.00	2,250.00	9,000.00	35.00	1,500.00
2002 (56th)	175.00	1,750.00	2,500.00	9,000.00	50.00	1,750.00

50-YEAR PRICE RANGE OF 16 SELECTED CANADIAN COINS (cont.)

	10 Cents 1889		20 Cents 1858		25 Cents 1875	
	VG	Unc	VG	Unc	VG	Unc
1952 (1st)	15.00	70.00	1.25	3.50	4.00	12.00
1953 (2nd)	30.00	75.00	1.75	5.50	15.00	40.00
1955 (3rd)	50.00	110.00	2.50	8.00	35.00	75.00
1956 (4th)	50.00	175.00	3.50	12.00	35.00	120.00
1957 (5th)	75.00	200.00	5.00	13.00	35.00	120.00
1958 (6th)	75.00	250.00	6.00	18.00	35.00	130.00
1959 (7th)	150.00	500.00	9.00	25.00	50.00	300.00
1960 (8th)	200.00	750.00	10.00	35.00	75.00	450.00
1961 (9th)	200.00	1,000.00	10.00	35.00	100.00	600.00
1962 (10th)	200.00	1,200.00	15.00	40.00	100.00	750.00
1963 (11th)	200.00	1,400.00	40.00	125.00	100.00	800.00
1964 (12th)	250.00	1,500.00	45.00	225.00	115.00	1,200.00
1965 (13th)	225.00	2,000.00	45.00	300.00	115.00	1,400.00
1966 (14th)	225.00	2,800.00	45.00	325.00	115.00	1,500.00
1967 (15th)	200.00	2,500.00	45.00	350.00	105.00	1,500.00
1968 (16th)	200.00	2,300.00	45.00	325.00	100.00	1,400.00
1969 (17th)	200.00	2,300.00	45.00	325.00	100.00	1,400.00
1970 (18th)	200.00	2,300.00	40.00	325.00	100.00	1,400.00
1971 (19th)	200.00	2,300.00	40.00	325.00	100.00	1,400.00
1972 (20th)	200.00	2,300.00	40.00	325.00	100.00	1,400.00
1973 (21st)	200.00	2,300.00	35.00	300.00	90.00	1,350.00
1974 (22nd)	200.00	2,300.00	35.00	275.00	80.00	1,500.00
1975 (23rd)	200.00	2,300.00	35.00	275.00	80.00	1,500.00
1976 (24th)	200.00	2,500.00	35.00	275.00	80.00	1,500.00
1977 (25th)	250.00	2,800.00	45.00	325.00	125.00	1,900.00
1979 (27th)	250.00	3,000.00	45.00	450.00	125.00	2,500.00
1980 (29th)	325.00	3,500.00	50.00	800.00	130.00	4,000.00
1981 (31st)	450.00	5,000.00	60.00	1,500.00	200.00	9,000.00
1982 (33rd)	450.00	10,500.00	65.00	1,600.00	200.00	9,000.00
1983 (35tht)	450.00	9,000.00	65.00	1,600.00	200.00	9,000.00
1984 (37th)	450.00	9,000.00	75.00	1,500.00	225.00	8,000.00
1985 (39th)	450.00	7,500.00	75.00	1,250.00	225.00	6,500.00
1987 (41st)	475.00	9,200.00	65.00	1,600.00	225.00	8,200.00
1989 (43rd)	490.00	9,300.00	65.00	1,600.00	250.00	8,000.00
1991 (45th)	500.00	8,500.00	70.00	1,600.00	250.00	7,000.00
1993 (47th)	500.00	—	70.00	1,200.00	275.00	7,500.00
1995 (49th)	600.00	10,000.00	75.00	1,200.00	350.00	7,500.00
1997 (51st)	650.00	15,000.00	75.00	1,200.00	350.00	15,000.00
1999 (53rd)	700.00	—	75.00	1,100.00	375.00	17,500.00
2002 (56th)	800.00	20,000.00	90.00	1,100.00	425.00	17,500.00

50-YEAR PRICE RANGE OF 16 SELECTED CANADIAN COINS (cont.)

	50 Cents 1921		50 Cents 1947 ML, Curved 7		Silver Dollar 1948	
	VG	Unc	VG	Unc	VG	Unc
1952 (1st)	50.00	200.00	.85	2.00	2.00	4.00
1953 (2nd)	100.00	400.00	5.00	10.00	2.50	5.00
1955 (3rd)	200.00	600.00	15.00	30.00	3.00	8.00
1956 (4th)	400.00	1,200.00	30.00	50.00	4.00	12.00
1957 (5th)	500.00	1,500.00	50.00	140.00	7.00	15.00
1958 (6th)	500.00	2,500.00	125.00	250.00	17.00	30.00
1959 (7th)	700.00	3,500.00	100.00	275.00	35.00	60.00
1960 (8th)	700.00	3,500.00	150.00	300.00	45.00	75.00
1961 (9th)	800.00	3,500.00	175.00	350.00	45.00	75.00
1962 (10th)	800.00	4,000.00	175.00	400.00	45.00	70.00
1963 (11th)	2,000.00	7,000.00	250.00	500.00	55.00	80.00
1964 (12th)	3,000.00	8,000.00	300.00	600.00	100.00	175.00
1965 (13th)	3,300.00	12,000.00	300.00	750.00	100.00	250.00
1966 (14th)	3,300.00	12,000.00	325.00	850.00	125.00	300.00
1967 (15th)	3,300.00	9,000.00	325.00	850.00	125.00	275.00
1968 (16th)	3,300.00	8,000.00	325.00	850.00	150.00	235.00
1969 (17th)	3,300.00	8,000.00	350.00	850.00	150.00	250.00
1970 (18th)	3,300.00	8,000.00	350.00	850.00	150.00	260.00
1971 (19th)	3,300.00	8,000.00	350.00	850.00	125.00	260.00
1972 (20th)	3,300.00	8,000.00	350.00	850.00	125.00	260.00
1973 (21st)	3,300.00	8,000.00	350.00	850.00	125.00	260.00
1974 (22nd)	3,000.00	8,000.00	400.00	900.00	150.00	300.00
1975 (23rd)	3,000.00	9,000.00	500.00	1,100.00	225.00	600.00
1976 (24th)	4,000.00	10,000.00	800.00	1,700.00	300.00	750.00
1977 (25th)	5,000.00	15,000.00	1,200.00	2,500.00	300.00	650.00
1979 (27th)	6,000.00	22,000.00	900.00	2,500.00	425.00	700.00
1980 (29th)	6,000.00	35,000.00	1,300.00	3,500.00	500.00	900.00
1981 (31st)	7,000.00	40,000.00	2,000.00	5,000.00	1,200.00	2,500.00
1982 (33rd)	7,000.00	40,000.00	2,000.00	5,000.00	900.00	2,000.00
1983 (35tht)	7,000.00	60,000.00	1,500.00	6,000.00	700.00	1,500.00
1984 (37th)	7,000.00	60,000.00	2,000.00	6,000.00	700.00	1,250.00
1985 (39th)	7,000.00	50,000.00	2,000.00	5,800.00	700.00	1,250.00
1987 (41st)	13,000.00	50,000.00	1,350.00	5,000.00	725.00	1,500.00
1989 (43rd)	15,000.00	—	1,350.00	5,000.00	800.00	1,500.00
1991 (45th)	15,000.00	—	2,200.00	4,500.00	800.00	1,200.00
1993 (47th)	11,000.00	40,000.00	1,800.00	5,000.00	800.00	1,200.00
1995 (49th)	13,000.00	40,000.00	1,800.00	5,000.00	850.00	1,250.00
1997 (51st)	13,500.00	45,000.00	1,800.00	5,000.00	850.00	1,000.00
1999 (53rd)	16,000.00	45,000.00	1,800.00	5,500.00	750.00	1,100.00
2002 (56th)	22,500.00	—	1,750.00	6,000.00	800.00	1,100.00

50-YEAR PRICE RANGE OF 16 SELECTED CANADIAN COINS (cont.)

	$5 Gold 1914		Sovereign 1908C		Newfoundland $2 Gold 1880	
	VG	Unc	VG	Unc	VG	Unc
1952 (1st)	18.00	23.00	40.00	55.00	30.00	45.00
1953 (2nd)	20.00	26.00	45.00	50.00	45.00	55.00
1955 (3rd)	30.00	35.00	75.00	100.00	70.00	90.00
1956 (4th)	30.00	40.00	100.00	125.00	80.00	125.00
1957 (5th)	30.00	40.00	100.00	125.00	125.00	175.00
1958 (6th)	50.00	75.00	100.00	125.00	200.00	300.00
1959 (7th)	100.00	125.00	100.00	125.00	250.00	400.00
1960 (8th)	125.00	200.00	100.00	125.00	300.00	450.00
1961 (9th)	175.00	225.00	150.00	200.00	300.00	500.00
1962 (10th)	200.00	250.00	200.00	300.00	350.00	550.00
1963 (11th)	225.00	275.00	350.00	500.00	350.00	550.00
1964 (12th)	225.00	325.00	600.00	800.00	350.00	550.00
1965 (13th)	225.00	325.00	600.00	900.00	350.00	550.00
1966 (14th)	225.00	325.00	600.00	900.00	350.00	550.00
1967 (15th)	250.00	325.00	600.00	900.00	350.00	550.00
1968 (16th)	250.00	325.00	600.00	800.00	350.00	550.00
1969 (17th)	250.00	350.00	600.00	800.00	350.00	550.00
1970 (18th)	250.00	355.00	600.00	800.00	350.00	550.00
1971 (19th)	250.00	355.00	600.00	800.00	350.00	550.00
1972 (20th)	250.00	355.00	550.00	800.00	350.00	550.00
1973 (21st)	200.00	325.00	550.00	800.00	350.00	600.00
1974 (22nd)	275.00	450.00	850.00	1,200.00	750.00	1,000.00
1975 (23rd)	350.00	550.00	850.00	1,200.00	750.00	1,000.00
1976 (24th)	400.00	700.00	850.00	1,200.00	800.00	1,500.00
1977 (25th)	425.00	750.00	1,200.00	2,000.00	900.00	1,600.00
1979 (27th)	425.00	650.00	1,200.00	2,000.00	900.00	2,000.00
1980 (29th)	600.00	1,000.00	1,200.00	2,200.00	1,000.00	2,200.00
1981 (31st)	900.00	1,300.00	2,000.00	4,000.00	1,800.00	3,500.00
1982 (33rd)	800.00	1,400.00	2,000.00	4,500.00	1,600.00	3,500.00
1983 (35tht)	600.00	1,300.00	1,000.00	2,500.00	1,600.00	5,000.00
1984 (37th)	500.00	1,200.00	2,000.00	4,500.00	2,200.00	6,000.00
1985 (39th)	500.00	1,200.00	2,000.00	4,500.00	2,200.00	5,000.00
1987 (41st)	585.00	1,265.00	2,750.00	4,250.00	2,200.00	8,000.00
1989 (43rd)	500.00	1,200.00	2,500.00	4,250.00	2,400.00	8,000.00
1991 (45th)	400.00	900.00	2,000.00	3,600.00	2,000.00	8,000.00
1993 (47th)	450.00	950.00	2,500.00	4,00000	1,700.00	7,500.00
1995 (49th)	450.00	1,250.00	2,750.00	5,000.00	1,700.00	7,500.00
1997 (51st)	450.00	1,250.00	2,750.00	4,000.00	1,700.00	7,500.00
1999 (53rd)	400.00	1,000.00	2,500.00	4,000.00	1,700.00	7,500.00
2002 (55th)	400.00	1,000.00	2,500.00	4,000.00	1,700.00	7,500.00

50-YEAR PRICE RANGE OF 16 SELECTED CANADIAN COINS (cont.)

Proof-Like
1954

	Set	Dollar
1952 (1st)		
1953 (2nd)		
1955 (3rd)		
1956 (4th)		
1957 (5th)		
1958 (6th)		
1959 (7th)	10.00	4.50
1960 (8th)	14.00	7.00
1961 (9th)	25.00	10.00
1962 (10th)	50.00	15.00
1963 (11th)	70.00	30.00
1964 (12th)	150.00	65.00
1965 (13th)	215.00	115.00
1966 (14th)	200.00	115.00
1967 (15th)	115.00	75.00
1968 (16th)	90.00	60.00
1969 (17th)	100.00	65.00
1970 (18th)	100.00	65.00
1971 (19th)	100.00	65.00
1972 (20th)	95.00	60.00
1973 (21st)	85.00	60.00
1974 (22nd)	100.00	75.00
1975 (23rd)	175.00	90.00
1976 (24th)	200.00	100.00
1977 (25th)	190.00	100.00
1979 (27th)	300.00	150.00
1980 (29th)	300.00	180.00
1981 (31st)	500.00	200.00
1982 (33rd)	450.00	200.00
1983 (35tht)	400.00	160.00
1984 (37th)	500.00	200.00
1985 (39th)	500.00	200.00
1987 (41st)	400.00	300.00
1989 (43rd)	400.00	300.00
1991 (45th)	400.00	300.00
1993 (47th)	350.00	200.00
1995 (49th)	350.00	175.00
1997 (51st)	260.00	175.00
1999 (53rd)	240.00	150.00
2002 (56th)	250.00	125.00

BIBLIOGRAPHY

1. "A Weekly Coin Paper: Proving Worth to Disbelievers. "*Coin World*, 25th Anniversary Supplement, 17 April 1985, pp. 2-7.

2. Aaron, Bob. "Tax Court Takes Collectors." In "Coin Commentary." *Canadian Coin News*, 28 April 1987, pp. 7, 16.

3. Allen, Harold Don. Canadian Coins are Top." *Star Weekly Magazine*, 29 March 1958, pp. 16-17.

4. _____. *Canadian Numismatic Digest* [compilation of 40 articles by the author]. Montreal: Robert Verity for National Coin Week Exhibition, Queen Elizabeth Hotel, and for Montreal Coin Club and Association des Numismates de Montréal, 1960, pp. vi + 74.

5. _____. "Changing Patterns in Canada's Currency, 1858-1958." *Canadian Numismatic Journal*, November 1958, pp. 336-341, and December 1958, pp. 367-376.

6. _____. "Coin Collecting Hits a New High." *Star Weekly Magazine*, 26 January 1957, pp. 30-31.

7. _____. "Een Nederlands perspectief bij verzamelen Canadees papiergeld." Translation into Dutch by Hans Hoogendoom. *'t Watermerk*. November 2000, cover, pp. 18-22.

8. _____. "Fifty-Year Reflection: A Good Time is Now." *Canadian Numismatic Journal*, March 2000, pp. 59-73.

9. _____. "Toward a Money Tomorrow: Numismatics is an Age of Paper and of Plastic." *Journal of International Numismatics*, Vol. 7 (1973), pp. 1-4, 21; 25-30, 43; 49-56.

10. "Armed Robbers Get $100,000 from Montreal Museum." *Canada Coin News*, 6 February 1965, p. 1.

11. Atkinson, William. "Jim Charlton Gives Back to Coin Hobby: Canadian Active at 80." *Coin World*, 22 May 1991, p. 68.

12. Bell, Geoffrey G. "Counterfeits, Customs & Strikes, 1975-79. [the period of the Charlton presidency]." In "Flashback — Reminiscences." *Canadian Numismatic Journal*, July-August 2000, pp. 267-269.

13. Bender, Eric. "Tried to Corner Market: Coin Speculators' Bankruptcy Called Boon to Collectors." *Ottawa Journal*, 1 September 1967, p. 32.

14. Boily, Raymond. *Monnaies, Médailles & Jetons au Canada*. Cahier de la Société Numismatique de Québec. Québec: The Society, 1980, pp. 87.

15. Bowers, Q. David. *The American Numismatic Association: Centennial History*. 2 vols. Wolfeboro, New Hampshire: Bowers and Merena Galleries, Inc., for the American Numismatic Association, 1991, pp. xi + 1744.

16. Bowman, Fred. "Communion Tokens of the Presbyterian Church of Canada." In 26 parts. Preface by J. Douglas Ferguson. *Canadian Numismatic Journal*, November 1962 through December 1964.

17. "CNA's Charlton Names Allen to Head 'Canadian Coin Week.'" *Coin World*, 9 November 1977, p. 3.

18. "Canada Coin Exchange Expands Wholesale, Retail Facilities." *Canadian Coin and Stamp World*, July 1963, p. 1.

19. "Canada Plans Complete Centennial Coin Issue." *Coin World*, 4 May 1966, p. 45.

20. "Canada Trends New Feature of Coin World." *Coin World*, 23 June 1961, pp. 1-2.

21. "Canadian Tax Court Rules Against Collectors." *Coin World*, 31 December 1986, p. 12.

22. "Century of Canadian Numismatics: History Traces Growth of Numismatics in Canada." *Coin World*, 14 April 1965, pp. 45-46.

23. Charlton, J. E. *1952 Catalogue of Canadian Coins, Tokens & Fractional Currency*. Toronto: The Author, 1952, pp. 34.

24. _____. *1966 Standard Catalogue of Canadian Coins, Tokens and Paper Money*. Fully illustrated, 1670 to Date. 14th edition. Racine, Wisconsin: Whitman Publishing Company, © 1965, pp. 127.

25. _____. *1971 Standard Catalogue of Canadian Coins, Tokens & Paper Money*. Fully illustrated, 1670 to Date.19th edition. Port Carling, Ontario: Charlton Publications, © 1970, pp. 200.

26. _____. *1978 Standard Catalogue of Canadian Coins, Tokens & Paper Money*. 26th edition. Toronto: Charlton International Publishing Inc., © 1977, pp. 341.

27. _____. "Early P-L Cuttoff Plea Rejected. In "Trends of Today's Canadian Coin Values." *Coin World*, 1 September 1965, p. 45.

28. _____. "History Traces Growth of Numismatics in Canada." *Coin World*, 14 April 1965, pp. 45, 50.

29. _____. "King of Canadian Coins." In "Money Talks." *Toronto Daily Star*, 7 February 1959, p. 56.

30. _____. "Profit-Taking Sags in Proof-Likes." In "Trends of Today's Canadian Coin Values." *Coin World*, 12 May 1965, p. 42.

31. Charlton, J. E. "Set Fiasco Yields Bitter Fruit." In "Trends of Today's Canadian Coin Values." *Coin World*, 3 February 1965, p. 46.

32. _____. "The Numismatic Treasures of 'Le Chameau.'" *Canadian Numismatic Journal*, September 1976, pp. 307-309.

33. _____. "Toronto Coin Club History Traced from Enthusiastic Beginning in '36: Big Membership Increase Began After World War II." *Coin World*, 28 June 1963, p. 35.

34. _____. "Honesty Best Response when Cherrypicking." In "Letters to the Editor." *Coin World*, 13 March 1995, p. 25.

35. _____. "O Canada: Wampum to Tokens, Beavers to Loons." *World Coins*, Special Monthly Supplement to *Coin World*, January 1988, pp. S-3 to S-41.

36. _____, and Robert C. Willey. *Standard Grading Guide to Canadian Decimal Coins*. Racine, Wisconsin: Whitman Publishing Company, © 1965, pp. 157.

37. "Charlton Responsible for Advancing Canadian Numismatics Around the World." Reprinted from *Numismatic News,* 8 February 2000. In "Spotlight on People." *Ontario Numismatist*, July-August 2000, pp. 98-99.

38. "Charlton Returns as Canadian Trends Editor." *Coin World*, 26 October 1983.

39. "Cherrypicking Ethics: Seller Beware or Honesty?" *Coin World*, 13 February 1995, p. 10.

40. *Coin & Stamp Collectors Accessories*. Toronto: Charlton Coin & Stamp Co., Ltd., n.d. [1967], pp. 44.

41. "Coin Investment New Science: Indiana Scientist Develops Plan to Pay Big Percentage: Harold Metcalf Convinces Bankers, Becomes Pioneer." *Coin World*, 13 July 1962, p. 48.

42. "Colville Designs Attract Criticism from Competitor." *Coin World*, 1 June 1966, p. 48.

43. Cross, W. K., publisher. *The 1997 Charlton Coin Guide*. Dealer's Buying Prices for Canadian, Newfoundland and Maritime Coinage, Canadian Medals, Tokens and Paper Money, United States and World Gold Coinage. 36th edition. Toronto, and Birmingham, Michigan: The Charlton Press, © 1996, pp. 112.

44. _____. *The Charlton Standard Catalogue of Canadian Bank Notes*. 3rd edition. Walter D. Allan, editor. Birmingham, Michigan, and Toronto: The Charlton Press, © 1996, pp. xi + 524.

45. Cross, W. K., *The Charlton Standard Catalogue of Canadian Government Paper Money*. Robert J. Graham, editor. Toronto, and Palm Harbor, Florida: The Charlton Press, © 2000, pp. xiv + 306.

46. _____. publisher and editor. *The Charlton Standard Catalogue of Canadian Coins*. 55th edition. Toronto, and Palm Harbor, Florida: The Charlton Press, © 2000, pp. xxxii + 320.

47. _____. *The Charlton Standard Catalogue of Canadian Colonial Tokens*. 2nd edition. Toronto: The Charlton Press, © 1990, pp. xii + 222.

48. _____. *The Charlton Standard Catalogue of Canadian Communion Tokens*. Introduction by Warren Baker. 2nd edition. Toronto, and Palm Harbor, Florida: The Charlton Press, © 2000, pp. xx + 284.

49. "Curator Lists Material Stolen During Armed Robbery of Museum [Chateau de Ramezay]." *Coin World*, 3 February 1965, p. 49.

50. Denison, Merrill. *Canada's First Bank: A History of the Bank of Montreal*. 2 vols. Toronto and Montreal: McClelland and Stewart, 1967, pp. xix + 471 + 453.

51. "Donation Gratefully Accepted." *Canadian Coin News*, 11 March 1980, p. 1.

52. "Expert Testimony Supports Conn's Valuations." *Coin World*, 21 November 1984, p. 12.

53. Ferguson, J. Douglas. "Numismatics Across Canada." *Canadian Numismatic Journal*, September 1965, pp. 357-358, and October 1965, pp. 405-407.

54. "Five Rules for Cherrypicking." *Coin World*, 13 February 1995, p. 10.

55. "Frank Rose Succeeds J. E. Charlton as Canadian Editor for Coin World." *Coin World*, 8 October 1969, p. 51.

56. Friedberg, Robert. *Paper Money of the United States*. A Complete Illustrated Guide with Valuations. 2nd edition. New York: Coin and Currency Publishing Institute, 1955, pp. vi +151.

57. Gibbs, William T. "Knowledge Essential Too for Plucking Cherry Coins: Know as Much as You Can and Win." *Coin World*, 13 February 1995, p. 10.

58. Graham, Robert J. "Jim Charlton Remembers." *Canadian Paper Money Society Newsletter*, November 1995, pp. 76-77.

59. Greene, Ronald. "Noted Numismatist Had a Life-Long Interest in Coins [obituary, Robert C. Willey]." *Canadian Coin News,* 1 February 1994, p. 25.

60. *Guide Officiel des Monnaies Canadiennes, 2001.* Toronto: Unitrade Press, © 2000, pp. 184.

61. Guren, Jay. "CW Readers Disagree with Designs Chosen for Centennial Coinage: Runnerup Designs Prove More Popular with Readers." *Coin World,* 8 February 1967, p. 48.

62. _____. "Confederation Competition Runnerup Claims Contest Spirit Abandonment." *Coin World,* 16 November 1966, pp. 47, 49.

63. Haxby, J. A., and R. C. Willey. *Coins of Canada.* 18th edition, 2000. Toronto: Unitrade Press, © 1999, pp. 282.

64. "Imperial [C.I.B.C.] Moves Display of Canadian Notes, Coins to Branch in Montreal." *Coin World,* 21 June 1967, pp. 41, 44.

65. Irwin, Ross W. In "Letter from our Members." *Canadian Numismatic Journal,* July-August 2000, pp. 265-266.

66. "J. E. Charlton Named to Edit Canada Section." *Coin World,* 3 May 1963, pp. 1-2.

67. Jarvis, Cale B. "Greater Toronto Exhibition Successful Three Day Event." *Coin World,* 14 December 1962, p. 54.

68. Kosoff, A. "Canada's Jim Charlton Followed Hobby from Youth into Professional Career." In "Kosoff Commentary." *Coin World,* 9 June 1976, pp. 46, 58.

69. Kumpikevicius, Gordon. "Many New Collectors Owe a Debt to Stan [biography, Stanley H. Clute]." In "Ancients." *Canadian Coin News,* 7 June 1994, pp. 8, 10.

70. *Le Catalogue Standard Charlton des Monnaies Canadiennes.* 50ième Edition Anniversaire. W. K. Cross, éditeur. Toronto, and Birmingham, Michigan: Charlton Press, © 1995, pp. xxxii + 271.

71. Lemke, Bob. *A Building is Only as Good as its Foundation: Krause Publications' Traditions and Philosophies at 45 Years.* Iola, Wisconsin: Krause Publications, 1997, pp. 302.

72. Lorimer, Donald C., publisher. *The Charlton Standard Catalogue of Canadian Government Paper Money.* Text by Robert J. Graham. 1st edition. Toronto: © The Charlton Press, 1984, pp. xxii + 259.

73. McCabe, L. W. "Coin of the Realm: A Commentary on Coinage by Tale, Currency by Tale, and the Qualities of Lawful Money." *Canadian Numismatic Journal,* August 1962, pp. 430-432; September 1962, pp. 469-472; October, pp. 503-505.

74. McCullough, A. B. *Money and Exchange in Canada to 1900*. Toronto and Charlottetown: Dundurn Press, in co-operation with Parks Canada and Canadian Government Publishing Centre, Supply and Services Canada, 1984, pp. 323.

75. McLachlan, R. W. "Some Reflections Upon Being Fifty Years a Coin Collector." Reprinted from *The Numismatist*, September 1911. *Canadian Numismatic Journal*, December 1961, pp. 516-518, and March 1962, pp. 144-149.

76. "Nickle Arts Museum Benefits from Donations." *Canadian Coin News*, 14 January 1980, p. 1.

77. "1911 Dollar Changes Hands, Comes Back to Canada." *Canadian Coin News*, 2 April 1985, p. 1.

78. "Numismatists Challenge Value of Donation." *Coin World*, 18 July 1984, p. 7.

79. "Ontario Numismatic Association Medallist of the Year: Mr. James E. Charlton." *Ontario Numismatist*, June 1967, p. 42.

80. "Ottawa Mint Plans Crash Program to Produce 1965 Proof-Like Sets: Finance Minister Promises Proof-Like Sets for All." *Canadian Coin News*, 20 February 1965, p. 1.

81. Pittman, Polly Edwards. "A Daughter's Tale: Integrity, Knowledge & Determination Guided Legendary John Jay Pittmam's Never-Ending Quest for Coins." *Coin World*, 8 September 1997, pp. 82-94.

82. "Rare 1911 $1 Fails to Sell." *Canadian Coin News*, 31 August 1993, p. 1.

83. "Record-Price Canadian Pattern Resold for Reported $135,000." *Coin World*, 3 November 1976, p. 3.

84. Rochette, Edward C. "The Man Who Wrote the Bible [biography, Richard S. Yeoman]." In "The Other Side of the Coin." *The Numismatist*, June 1987, pp. 1257-59.

85. "Rose, Canadian Trends Editor, Dies." *Coin World*, 4 May 1983, p. 3.

86. Schreiner, Jack. "Here's a Mint Condition Epidemic: Soon Have Wire Service for Our Coin Collectors." *Financial Post*, 20 April 1963, p. 14.

87. Schull, Joseph, and J. Douglas Gibson. *The Scotiabank Story*. A History of the Bank of Nova Scotia, 1832-1982. Toronto: Macmillan of Canada, A Division of Gage Publishing Limited, © 1982, pp. xvi + 421.

88. "Summer Coin Fair Successful!" *Canadian Coin News*, 4 August 1987, p. 1.

89. Taylor, H. C., and Somer James. *1960-61 Guide Book of Canadian Coins, Currency and Tokens.* Fully illustrated. 2nd edition, revised and enlarged. Winnipeg: Canadian Numismatic Publishing Institute, © 1960, pp. 232.

90. "The Problem of Buying." *C.N.A. Bulletin*, March 1950, p. 5.

91. "Thief Catcher Nabs Two Men." *Toronto Star*, 22 September 1958.

92. Thomas, Don. "Canada's Coin Bible [the Charlton catalogue]." In "Don Thomas, Publisher."*Canadian Coin News*, 2 August 1976, p. 4.

93. "2 Tried Crime to Pay Debts, Get 5, 3 Years." *Toronto Globe and Mail*, 21 October 1958, p. 5.

94. "UTC [United Teletype Coin Exchange Circuit] Folds in Canada." *Coin World*, 16 November 1966, p. 47.

95. Waring, Beth. "How to Get Rich Quick — On Nickels: Buy a Sackful of New Ones from Ottawa and Sit Tight." *Maclean's Reports*, 2 January 1965, p. 3.

96. "Whitman Releases Revised Charlton Work on Canada Coins, Tokens, Paper." *Coin World*, 8 October 1969, p. 53.

97. Willey, Robert. "The C.N.A.: 25 Years of Growth and Dedicated Individuals." *Coin Stamp Antique News*, 19 July 1975, pp. 12-18.

98. "World Coins, Scrapbook Merge in expanded Coin World Format." *Coin World*, 11 February 1976, pp. 1, 3.

99. Yeoman, R. S. *A Guide Book of United States Coins.* Racine, Wisconsin: Whitman Publishing Company, © 1958, pp. 255.

100. Young, Scott. "The Day the Ottawa Mint Ran Out of Money." Reprinted from the *Globe and Mail. Canadian Coin News*, 6 February 1965, pp. 10, 19.